Kaplan Publishing are constantly finding new ways to support students looking for exam success and our online resources really do add an extra dimension to your studies.

This book comes with free MyKaplan online resources so that you can study anytime, anywhere. **This free online resource is not sold separately and is included in the price of the book.**

Having purchased this book, you have access to the following online study materials:

CONTENT	AAT	
	Text	Kit
Electronic version of the book	✓	✓
Knowledge Check tests with instant answers	✓	
Mock assessments online	✓	✓
Material updates	✓	✓

How to access your online resources

Received this book as part of your Kaplan course?
If you have a MyKaplan account, your full online resources will be added automatically, in line with the information in your course confirmation email. If you've not used MyKaplan before, you'll be sent an activation email once your resources are ready.

Bought your book from Kaplan?
We'll automatically add your online resources to your MyKaplan account. If you've not used MyKaplan before, you'll be sent an activation email.

Bought your book from elsewhere?
Go to **www.mykaplan.co.uk/add-online-resources**
Enter the ISBN number found on the title page and back cover of this book.
Add the unique pass key number contained in the scratch panel below.
You may be required to enter additional information during this process to set up or confirm your account details.

This code can only be used once for the registration of this book online. This registration and your online content will expire when the examinations covered by this book have taken place. Please allow one hour from the time you submit your book details for us to process your request.

Please scratch the film to access your unique code.

Please be aware that this code is case-sensitive and you will need to include the dashes within the passcode, but not when entering the ISBN.

AAT

Q2022

Business Awareness

EXAM KIT

This Exam Kit supports study for the following AAT qualifications:
AAT Level 3 Diploma in Accounting
AAT Level 3 Certificate in Bookkeeping
AAT Diploma in Accounting at SCQF Level 7

PUBLISHING

AAT: BUSINESS AWARENESS

British Library Cataloguing-in-Publication Data

A catalogue record for this book is available from the British Library.

Published by:

Kaplan Publishing UK

Unit 2 The Business Centre

Molly Millar's Lane

Wokingham

Berkshire

RG41 2QZ

ISBN: 978-1-83996-889-1

© Kaplan Financial Limited, 2024

Printed and bound in Great Britain

The text in this material and any others made available by any Kaplan Group company does not amount to advice on a particular matter and should not be taken as such. No reliance should be placed on the content as the basis for any investment or other decision or in connection with any advice given to third parties. Please consult your appropriate professional adviser as necessary. Kaplan Publishing Limited and all other Kaplan group companies expressly disclaim all liability to any person in respect of any losses or other claims, whether direct, indirect, incidental, consequential or otherwise arising in relation to the use of such materials.

All rights reserved. No part of this examination may be reproduced or transmitted in any form or by any means, electronic or mechanical, including photocopying, recording, or by any information storage and retrieval system, without prior permission from Kaplan Publishing.

This Product includes content from the International Auditing and Assurance Standards Board (IAASB) and the International Ethics Standards Board for Accountants (IESBA), published by the International Federation of Accountants (IFAC) in 2015 and is used with permission of IFAC.

CONTENTS

	Page
Unit specific information	P.4
Index to questions and answers	P.5
Exam technique	P.6
Kaplan's recommended revision approach	P.7

Practice questions	1
Answers to practice questions	77
Mock assessment questions	159
Answers to mock assessment questions	175

Features in this revision kit

In addition to providing a wide ranging bank of real exam style questions, we have also included in this kit:

- unit specific information and advice on exam technique
- our recommended approach to make your revision for this particular subject as effective as possible.

You will find a wealth of other resources to help you with your studies on the AAT website:

www.aat.org.uk/

Quality and accuracy are of the utmost importance to us so if you spot an error in any of our products, please send an email to mykaplanreporting@kaplan.com with full details, or follow the link to the feedback form in MyKaplan.

Our Quality Co-ordinator will work with our technical team to verify the error and take action to ensure it is corrected in future editions.

UNIT SPECIFIC INFORMATION

THE EXAM

FORMAT OF THE ASSESSMENT

The sample assessment consisted of seven independent tasks and it is expected that the real assessment will follow this structure. Three of the tasks will be human marked. Students will normally be assessed by computer-based assessment.

In any one assessment, students may not be assessed on all content, or on the full depth or breadth of a piece of content. The content assessed may change over time to ensure validity of assessment, but all assessment criteria will be tested over time.

The learning outcomes for this unit are as follows:

	Learning outcome	Weighting
1	Understand business types, structures and governance, and the legal framework in which they operate	25%
2	Understand the impact of the external and internal environment on businesses, their performance and decisions	20%
3	Understand how businesses and accountants comply with principles of professional ethics	20%
4	Understand the impact of new technologies in accounting and the risks associated with data security	15%
5	Communicate information to stakeholders	20%
	Total	100%

Time allowed

2 ½ hours

PASS MARK

The pass mark for all AAT CBAs is 70%.

 Always keep your eye on the clock and make sure you attempt all questions!

DETAILED SYLLABUS

The detailed syllabus and study guide written by the AAT can be found at:

www.aat.org.uk/

INDEX TO QUESTIONS AND ANSWERS

		Page number	
		Question	Answer
THE BUSINESS ORGANISATION			
1 – 12	Types of organisations	1	77
13 – 17	Governance	4	81
18 – 26	Types of funding used by businesses	5	83
27 – 29	Service businesses	7	86
THE LEGAL FRAMEWORK			
30 – 36	Regulation of companies	8	87
37 – 38	The rights and roles of shareholders	10	90
39 – 49	The role and duties of directors	11	90
50 – 58	Unlimited liability partnerships	13	93
STAKEHOLDERS			
59 – 70	Stakeholders	16	96
ORGANISATIONAL STRUCTURE			
71 – 84	Organisational structure and governance	20	100
85 – 96	The role of the finance function	24	104
97 – 110	Risk	27	108
EXTERNAL ANALYSIS			
111 – 120	PESTLE	32	113
121 – 132	The micro-economic environment	36	119
133 – 144	Sustainability	40	127
ETHICS			
145 – 156	Ethics	44	128
157 – 162	Money Laundering	50	133
TECHNOLOGY AFFECTING BUSINESS			
163 – 180	Technology	54	136
181 – 185	Data protection	59	142
186 – 196	Information-security and cyber-security	60	144
197 – 209	Information and big data	64	148
COMMUNICATING INFORMATION			
210 – 225	Visualising and communicating information	68	153
MOCK EXAM			
Questions and answers		159	175

EXAM TECHNIQUE

- **Do not skip any of the material** in the syllabus.
- **Read each question** *very* carefully.
- **Double-check your answer** before committing yourself to it.
- Answer **every** question – if you do not know an answer to a multiple choice question or true/false question, you don't lose anything by guessing. Think carefully before you **guess**.
- If you are answering a multiple-choice question, **eliminate first those answers that you know are wrong**. Then choose the most appropriate answer from those that are left.
- **Don't panic** if you realise you've answered a question incorrectly. Getting one question wrong will not mean the difference between passing and failing.

Computer-based exams – tips

- Do not attempt a CBA until you have **completed all study material** relating to it.
- On the AAT website there is a CBA demonstration. It is **ESSENTIAL** that you attempt this before your real CBA. You will become familiar with how to move around the CBA screens and the way that questions are formatted, increasing your confidence and speed in the actual exam.
- Be sure you understand how to use the **software** before you start the exam. If in doubt, ask the assessment centre staff to explain it to you.
- Questions are **displayed on the screen** and answers are entered using keyboard and mouse. At the end of the exam, you are given a certificate showing the result you have achieved.
- In addition to the traditional multiple-choice question type, CBAs will also contain **other types of questions**, such as number entry questions, drag and drop, true/false, pick lists or drop down menus or hybrids of these.
- You need to be sure you **know how to answer questions** of this type before you sit the exam, through practice.

KAPLAN'S RECOMMENDED REVISION APPROACH

QUESTION PRACTICE IS THE KEY TO SUCCESS

Success in professional examinations relies upon you acquiring a firm grasp of the required knowledge at the tuition phase. In order to be able to do the questions, knowledge is essential.

However, the difference between success and failure often hinges on your exam technique on the day and making the most of the revision phase of your studies.

The **Kaplan textbook** is the starting point, designed to provide the underpinning knowledge to tackle all questions. However, in the revision phase, poring over text books is not the answer.

Kaplan pocket notes are designed to help you quickly revise a topic area; however you then need to practise questions. There is a need to progress to exam style questions as soon as possible, and to tie your exam technique and technical knowledge together.

The importance of question practice cannot be over-emphasised.

The recommended approach below is designed by expert tutors in the field, in conjunction with their knowledge of the examiner and the specimen assessment.

You need to practise as many questions as possible in the time you have left.

OUR AIM

Our aim is to get you to the stage where you can attempt exam questions confidently, to time, in a closed book environment, with no supplementary help (i.e. to simulate the real examination experience).

Practising your exam technique is also vitally important for you to assess your progress and identify areas of weakness that may need more attention in the final run up to the examination.

In order to achieve this we recognise that initially you may feel the need to practice some questions with open book help.

Good exam technique is vital.

THE KAPLAN REVISION PLAN

Stage 1: Assess areas of strengths and weaknesses

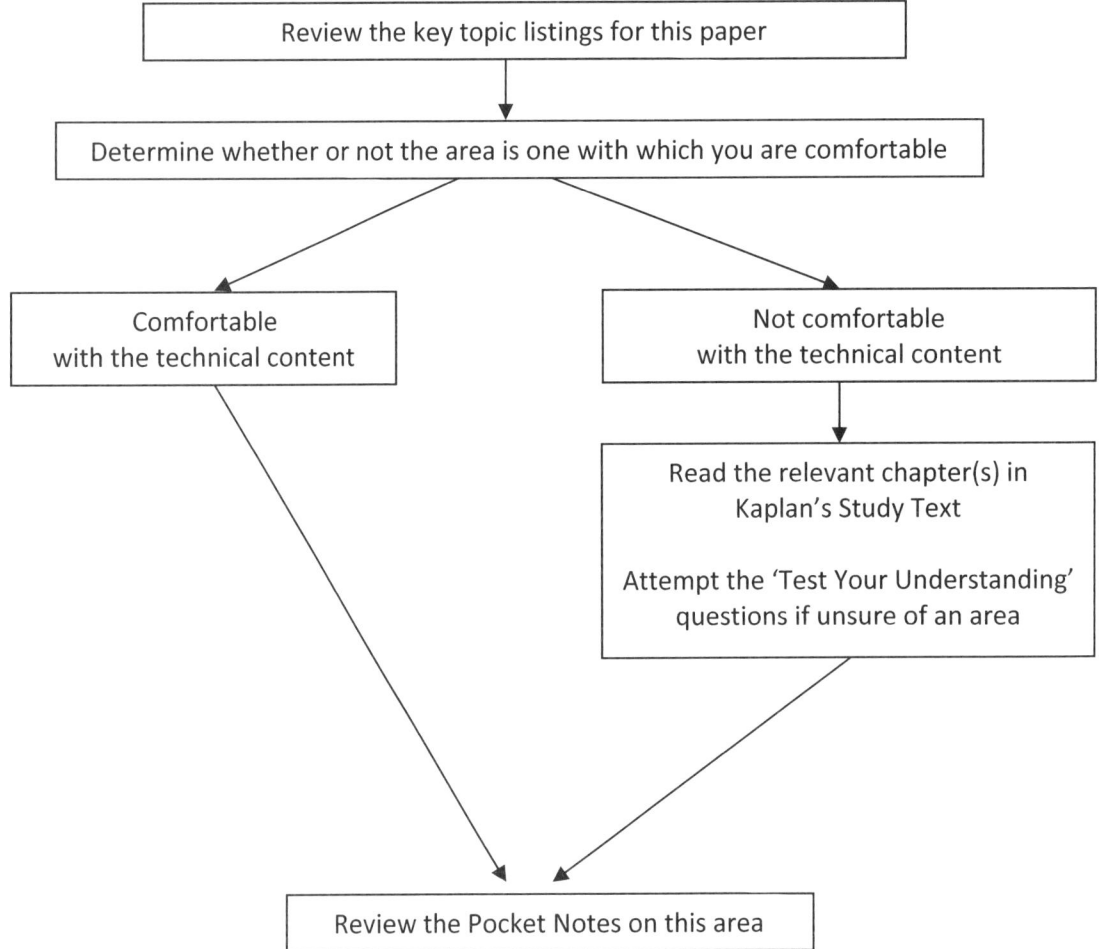

Stage 2: Practise questions

Follow the order of revision of topics as presented in this kit and attempt the questions in the order suggested.

Try to avoid referring to text books and notes and the model answer until you have completed your attempt.

Review your attempt with the model answer and assess how much of the answer you achieved.

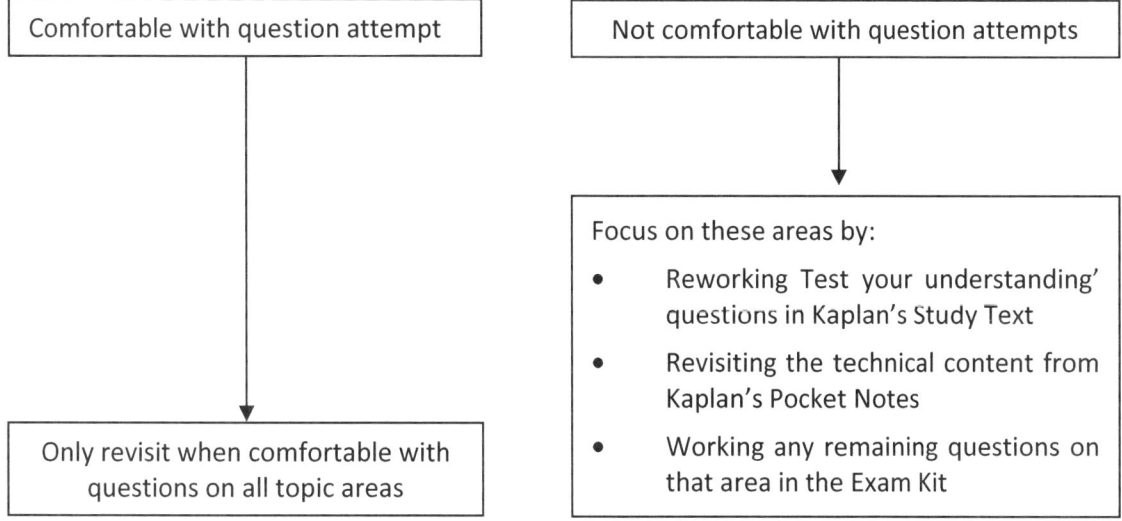

Stage 3: Final pre-exam revision

We recommend that you **attempt at least one two and a half hour mock examination** containing a set of previously unseen exam standard questions.

Attempt the mock CBA online in timed, closed book conditions to simulate the real exam experience.

Section 1

PRACTICE QUESTIONS

THE BUSINESS ORGANISATION

TYPES OF ORGANISATIONS

1   Which of the following is NOT a key feature of an organisation?

	✓
Controlled performance	
Collective goals	
Social arrangements	
Creation of a tangible product	

2   Which ONE of the following organisations is normally found in the public sector?

	✓
Schools	
Charities	
Clubs	
Businesses	

3   The public sector is normally concerned with which ONE of the following objectives?

	✓
Making profit from the sale of goods	
Providing services to specific groups funded from charitable donations	
The provision of basic government services	
Raising funds by subscriptions from members to provide common services	

AAT: BUSINESS AWARENESS

4 Which ONE of these organisations would normally be classified as BOTH a not-for-profit organisation AND a private sector organisation?

	✓
Government departments	
Partnerships	
Charities	
Companies	

5 A Ltd is a company that specialises in forestry. It has recently purchased B Ltd, which runs a chain of recreational resorts. A has allowed B to build several new resorts on land which is owned by A, but which it is no longer able to use. The resorts have proven highly profitable and popular.

Which ONE of the following best explains the reason for the improved performance of the combined entity?

	✓
Specialisation	
Social interactivity	
Synergy	
Service	

6 Identify whether each of the following statements is TRUE or FALSE.

Statement	True	False
Public limited companies are only owned by pension funds, trusts and other companies.		
A sole trader has unlimited personal liability for business debts.		

7 Identify whether each of the following statements is TRUE or FALSE.

Statement	True	False
Public limited companies have access to a wider pool of finance than partnerships or sole traders.		
Both public and private limited companies are allowed to sell shares to the public.		

8 Identify whether each of the following statements is TRUE or FALSE.

Statement	True	False
Companies are always owned by many different investors.		
Shareholders are liable for any debts the company may incur.		

PRACTICE QUESTIONS: SECTION 1

9 Identify whether each of the following statements is TRUE or FALSE.

Statement	True	False
Not-for-profit organisations (NFPs) have varied objectives, which depend on the needs of their members or the sections of society they were created to benefit.		
The primary objective of government-funded organisations is to reduce costs of their operations and thus minimise the burden on tax payers.		
Charities would usually be classified as a type of non-governmental organisation (NGO).		

10 Identify the correct type of organisation described in each of the following statements.

Statement	Sole trader	Public limited company	Unlimited liability partnership	Not-for-profit organisation
Owned by the shareholder(s)				
The multiple owners have personal liability for business debts				
Main objective is the provision of a service				
Can raise funds by issuing shares to the public				

11 Identify the correct type of organisation described in each of the following statements.

Statement	Sole trader	Public limited company	Limited liability partnership	Not-for-profit organisation
May be financed via subscriptions by members				
The single owner has personal liability for business debts				
Most likely to experience a separation between ownership and control				

12 Identify whether each of the following statements concerning sole traders is TRUE or FALSE.

Statement	True	False
The owner must do all the work		
The owner has limited liability for unpaid business debts		
The business may borrow money using the sole trader's assets as security		
The business has perpetual succession		

GOVERNANCE

13 Where there are a large number of external shareholders who play no role in the day-to-day running of a company, there is a situation that is described as:

	✓
Detached corporate ownership	
Uninvolved external ownership	
Dividend based shareholding	
Separation of ownership and control	

14 The system of policies by which an organisation is directed and controlled is known as which ONE of the following?

	✓
Corporate governance	
Corporate social responsibility	
Corporate infrastructure	
Corporate strategic apex	

15 Which ONE of the following is NOT a benefit of corporate governance?

	✓
Improved access to capital markets	
Stimulation of performance	
Enhanced marketability of goods and services	
Prevention of fraudulent claims by contractors	

16 Which ONE of the following is NOT normally seen to be an objective of corporate governance?

	✓
Improving employee welfare	
Increasing disclosure to stakeholders	
Ensuring that the company is run in a legal and ethical manner	
Increasing the level of confidence in the company for investors and shareholders	

17 The 'agency problem' refers to which ONE of the following situations?

	✓
Shareholders acting in their own short-term interests rather than the long-term interests of the company	
A vocal minority of shareholders expecting the directors to act as their agents and pay substantial dividends	
Companies reliant upon substantial government contracts such that they are effectively agents of the government	
The directors acting in their own interests rather than the shareholders' interests	

TYPES OF FUNDING USED BY BUSINESSES

18 Identify the type of funding most likely to be described in each of the following situations.

	New capital introduced	Working capital	Loan	Retained profits
A project is financed by cutting a dividend				
A new partner is accepted into a partnership				

19 Identify the type of funding most likely to be described in each of the following situations.

	New capital introduced	Working capital	Loan	Retained profits
A company delays paying suppliers				
A finance package involves monthly interest payments				

20 Fulling plc is considering asking for an extension to its overdraft facility. While most directors are in favour, the chairman is concerned about this plan.

Identify whether each of the following statements made by the Chairman is TRUE or FALSE.

Statement by Chairman	True	False
"I don't think we should extend our overdraft facility as interest must be paid on the full amount"		
"The overdraft is repayable on demand making it a risky method of finance"		

21 Westeros is an organisation which imports computers into country A and sells them the public in order to make a profit. It is owned by fifteen individual investors, each of whom owns an equal number of shares in Westeros. Westeros is not a public limited company.

Which of the following is likely to be the most appropriate source of finance for Westeros?

	✓
Central government funding	
The existing owners of Westeros	
Issue of shares to the public	
Donations from the public	

22 For each of the following financing scenarios, identify whether the funding suggested would be appropriate.

Scenario	Funding	Appropriate?
A Ltd is looking to buy land and build a new factory.	Working capital	
B Ltd is planning on investing in new plant and machinery to extend its production capacity to meet rising demand for its products.	Bank loan	

23 For each of the following financing scenarios, identify whether the funding suggested would be appropriate.

Scenario	Funding	Appropriate?
C Ltd has produced a cash flow forecast and has identified it will have a cash shortage for a two month period.	New share issue	
D Ltd has reached its overdraft limit but still needs finance to buy a rival company.	Retained earnings	

PRACTICE QUESTIONS: SECTION 1

24 For each of the following financing scenarios, identify whether the funding suggested would be appropriate.

Scenario	Funding	Appropriate?
ABC partnership wishes to buy a new building.	New share issue	
X, a sole trader, needs to buy new fixtures and fittings.	New capital introduced	

25 G Ltd is considering raising finance to invest in new premises. It believes that it should raise debt finance by way of a bank loan rather than a share issue.

Identify whether each of the following statements is TRUE or FALSE.

	True	False
Interest payments on a loan can be suspended in the future if G is unable to afford them.		
Dividends are an allowable deduction against G's profits.		
G will likely need to provide asset security to investors whether it chooses to raise debt or equity finance.		

26 Which ONE of the following sources of finance to companies is the most widely used in practice?

	✓
Bank borrowings	
Rights issues	
New share issues	
Retained earnings	

SERVICE BUSINESSES

27 Identify which quality of a service is described in each of the following statements.

Statement	Intangibility	Simultaneity	Heterogeneity	Perishability
The consumption of a service happens at the same time as the service delivery.				
The quality of a service is harder to standardise, due to the person delivering the service.				
A service does not, in itself, give the customer a physical product.				
A service cannot be held in inventory to be used later when needed.				

28 VC Co is a firm of opticians. It provides a range of services to the public, such as eye tests and contact lens consultations, and has a separate dispensary selling glasses and contact lenses. Patients book appointments with an optician in advance.

A standard appointment is 30 minutes long, during which an optician will assess the patient's specific requirements and provide them with the eye care services they need.

Which of the following describes a characteristic of the services provided by an optician at VC Co during a standard appointment?

	✓
Tangible	
Homogeneous	
Non-perishable	
Simultaneous	

29 United Training Ltd is a training organisation that offers a wide range of business courses in areas such as accountancy, marketing and HR. Recent learner feedback has highlighted significant differences in the perceived quality of different lecturers.

Identify whether each of the following statements regarding United Training Ltd is TRUE or FALSE.

	True	False
It is more difficult to measure the quality of lecturers than it is to asses a physical product.		
Effective staff recruitment and training are key ways of trying to ensure quality within United Training Ltd.		
There is unlikely to be a link between staff utilisation and the perceived quality of courses.		

THE LEGAL FRAMEWORK

REGULATION OF COMPANIES

30 **Identify whether each of the following statements about the financial statements of limited companies is TRUE or FALSE.**

	True	False
Financial statements should give a "true and fair" view of the position and performance of the company.		
The term "true and fair" is precisely defined in UK company law.		

31 Identify whether each of the following statements about the financial statements of limited companies is TRUE or FALSE.

	True	False
Companies are not required by law to maintain proper accounting records but do so because it is good practice.		
The detailed content and specification of "proper accounting records" is precisely defined in UK company law.		

32 Identify whether each of the following statements about the financial statements of limited companies is TRUE or FALSE.

	True	False
Shareholders are responsible for the preparation of financial statements.		
Directors are responsible for the preparation of financial statements.		
Auditors are responsible for the preparation of financial statements.		
Financial statements must be approved by the board of directors.		

33 Which ONE of the following parties has primary responsibility for ensuring that the financial statements of a limited company give a "true and fair" view?

	✓
Directors	
Chief accountant	
Auditors	
Everyone working in the finance department	

34 Which ONE of the following characteristics of financial statements of a limited company is NOT normally required to ensure a "true and fair view"?

	✓
Does not contain any material misstatement	
Is 100% accurate	
Applies appropriate accounting standards	

35 A company is a separate legal entity to its shareholders and directors.

Which of the following are consequences of separate legal entity?

(1) A company is fully liable for its own debts.

(2) A company owns its own property.

(3) A company enters into contracts in its own name.

	✓
(1) and (2) only	
(1) and (3) only	
(2) and (3) only	
(1), (2) and (3)	

36 There are a number of important legal differences between unincorporated businesses (e.g. partnerships), and incorporated businesses (e.g. companies).

Which of the following are characteristics of a COMPANY?

(1) A company has perpetual succession.

(2) A company is subject to the requirements of the Companies Act 2006.

(3) There is no separation of ownership and management in a company.

	✓
(1) and (2) only	
(1) and (3) only	
(2) and (3) only	
(1), (2) and (3)	

THE RIGHTS AND ROLES OF SHAREHOLDERS

37 Which ONE of the following is known as the system of that directs and controls the way in which a company is operated?

	✓
Companies Act 2006	
Corporate Governance	
Centralised Control	
Mission Statement	

PRACTICE QUESTIONS: SECTION 1

38 Which ONE of the following is NOT a right of a shareholder?

	✓
To appoint a proxy	
To bring a derivative claim	
To vote on certain company affairs	
To recruit all members of staff	

THE ROLE AND DUTIES OF DIRECTORS

39 Jess sits on the board of directors, but is part time and isn't involved in the day to day running of the company.

Which ONE of the following descriptions best describes what type of director Jess is?

	✓
An executive director	
A non-executive director	
A part-time director	
Not any type of director	

40 Which ONE of the following is NOT a type of company director?

	✓
A supreme director	
A managing director	
An executive director	

41 What is the minimum age of a director as required by Companies Act 2006?

	✓
16	
18	
21	

42 To whom does a director owe their statutory duties to?

	✓
The members	
The board of directors	
The company as a whole	

43 Which ONE of the following describes a director with day to day responsibility for running a company?

	✓
Chairman of the Board	
President	
Managing Director	

44 Rebecca is appointed director of Blue Ltd, and given ultimate control over the day-to-day management of the company.

In the context of company law, what is Rebecca considered to be?

	✓
Managing director	
Operational manager	
Non-executive director	
Chairman	

45 Identify whether each of the following statements about directors is TRUE or FALSE.

	True	False
The statutory duty of a director to disclose any interest that they have in a proposed transaction or arrangement with the company does not apply to non-executive directors.		
A director may not exercise their powers except for the purpose for which they were conferred.		

46 Which TWO of the following are statutory duties of a director?

	✓
To promote the success of the company	
To promote the relationship between directors and employees	
To declare trading losses to members	
To declare an interest in an existing transaction or arrangement	

47 In company law, which ONE of the following is NOT a statutory duty of directors?

	✓
Duty to act within their powers	
Duty to exercise independent judgement	
Duty to avoid conflicts of interest	
Duty to protect shareholder value	

PRACTICE QUESTIONS: SECTION 1

48 Identify whether each of the following statements about directors is TRUE or FALSE.

	True	False
Directors' service contracts lasting more than one year must be approved by the members.		
Authority that flows for a person's position is known as "express" authority.		

49 Sam, a director of Aspic Ltd, is in breach of their statutory duties.

Identify whether each of the following statements about directors is TRUE or FALSE.

	True	False
Directors owe their duties to the company as a whole, not to individual members.		
The director may be required to make good any loss suffered by the company.		
Any property taken by the director from the company can be recovered from them if it is still in their possession.		

UNLIMITED LIABILITY PARTNERSHIPS

50 There are a number of important legal differences between companies and partnerships.

Identify whether each of the following statements concerning partnerships is TRUE or FALSE.

	True	False
There no formality required to create a partnership.		
Partners in a partnership are personally liable for the debts of the firm.		
Partnerships are not legally required to disclose their financial results to the general public.		

51 Which ONE of the following is required to establish an unlimited partnership?

	✓
The partners obtain permission through Companies Act 2006	
The partners obtain permission from Companies House	
The partners simply agree to form the partnership	

52 There are a number of important legal differences between companies and partnerships.

Identify whether each of the following statements is TRUE or FALSE.

	True	False
The partners in an ordinary partnership jointly own the firm's assets.		
The shareholders in a company jointly own the company's assets.		

53 Karishma owns a newsagent, runs it as the manager and employs Tessa as part-time help during the week. Karishma is fully liable for the business' debts.

What type of business does Karishma own?

	✓
Sole trader	
Limited company	
Partnership	

54 Identify whether each of the following statements is TRUE or FALSE.

	True	False
The directors of a company are liable for any losses of the company.		
A sole trader business is owned by shareholders and operated by the proprietor.		
Partners are liable for losses in a partnership in proportion to their profit share ratio.		
A company is run by directors on behalf of its members.		

55 Identify whether each of the following statements is TRUE or FALSE.

	True	False
A partnership is a separate legal entity.		
A partnership is jointly owned and managed by the partners.		
A partnership can raise capital by issuing shares to members of the public.		
A partnership is able to own property and other assets in its own name.		

PRACTICE QUESTIONS: SECTION 1

56 Identify whether each of the following statements relating to a partnership of twenty persons and a limited liability company with twenty shareholders, each with a five per cent shareholding, is TRUE or FALSE.

	True	False
Both partnerships and limited liability companies are able to own assets in their own name.		
The members of a limited liability company have the right to participate in the management of that company, whereas partners do not have the right to participate in the management of their partnership.		
The partners have the right to participate in the management of the partnership, whereas members of a limited liability company do not have the right to participate in the management of that company.		
Partnerships are subject to the same regulations regarding introduction and withdrawal of capital from the business as a limited liability company.		

57 Which of the following pairs of items would you expect to see in the financial statements of a partnership?

	✓
Dividends paid and Share premium account	
Capital accounts and Profit appropriation account	
Profit appropriation account and Dividends paid	
Share premium account and Capital accounts	

58 J, L and C are in partnership together running a farm, under the name Top Farm & Co. J enters into a contract to buy 20 sheep from Farms R Us for the farm. When L and C find out about this, they refuse to recognise the contract as all three partners had previously agreed not to buy any more animals for the next 3 months due to cash flow problems. J argues that the deal was too good to miss.

Which ONE of the following statements best summarises the legal position relating to the contract with Farms R Us?

	✓
J alone is liable because they acted without the other partners' authority.	
J, L and C are each personally liable, since partners are agents of each other.	
Top Farm & Co is liable as it was a contract entered into for the purposes of the partnership business.	
The firm and, therefore, all of its partners are liable on the contract to purchase 20 sheep from Farms R Us.	

STAKEHOLDERS

STAKEHOLDERS

59 Which THREE of the following would be considered to be connected stakeholders?

	✓
Employees	
Government	
Environmental pressure groups	
Suppliers	
Customers	
Lenders	

60 What are the three classifications of stakeholders commonly known as?

	✓
Internal, external, connected	
Shareholders, employees, customers	
Internal, external, regulated	
Connected, unconnected, external	

61 According to Mendelow, the significance of each stakeholder group in an organisation depends on two factors: the power of the stakeholder and the level of interest of the stakeholder.

		Interest	
		Low	High
Power	Low	I	II
	High	III	IV

What approach is recommended for dealing with stakeholders in quadrant III of the above matrix?

	✓
Develop strategies that are fully acceptable to the stakeholder	
Keep the stakeholder satisfied	
Keep the stakeholder informed	
Minimum effort	

62 BetWalt, a medium-sized online gambling company, is to move all of its operations from the UK to a different country to reduce its cost base.

In respect of this move, which ONE stakeholder group from the following list would need to be kept informed?

	✓
Low-skilled employees (not heavily unionised)	
Customers (both UK and abroad)	
UK government (BetWalt's move is not against local laws)	
Major institutional investors (with shareholdings of between 25% and 30% each)	

63 Employees are _____ stakeholders, while finance providers are _____ stakeholders.

Which two words fill the gaps in the above sentence?

GAP 1
Internal
External
Connected

GAP 2
Internal
Outsiders
Connected
Suppliers

64 A is a large company whose shares are owned by a large number of individual investors, who do not wish to engage with company's decision making despite having full rights to do so.

Using Mendelow's matrix, identify which ONE of the following responses would be appropriate for this stakeholder group.

	✓
Minimal effort	
Keep informed	
Keep satisfied	
Key players	

65 Identify whether the following statement is TRUE or FALSE.

Statement	True	False
A company is using a communication strategy aimed at explaining the rationale behind its actions to its stakeholders. Using Mendelow's matrix, these stakeholders would be categorised as 'minimal effort'.		

AAT: BUSINESS AWARENESS

66 Identify whether the following statement is TRUE or FALSE.

Statement	True	False
The interests of customers and shareholders can often appear to conflict – for example in the quality of goods and services.		

67 FFD plc is a large national manufacturer of animal feed based in country T. FFD sells dried food – primarily for chickens and sheep. This is not a competitive market and FFD's large number of small farmer customers have little alternative but to purchase FFD's products for their animals. The farming industry is struggling in country T with farmers earning very low margins and many being forced out of business.

The Government of country T has publically expressed concerns about the state of the national farming industry and has vowed to do whatever is necessary to protect farmers from what one minister has referred to as 'money-making corporations that are making excessive profits from farmers.'

FFD's shares are mainly held by individual investors – many of whom have invested a significant amount of money into FFD. However, no individual shareholder in FFD has more than 4% of the total share capital of the company.

FFD's employees are largely unskilled and are not members of any union.

FFD is currently considering raising its prices by around 15% to improve its margins. It has identified four main stakeholder groups who may be affected by the decision.

For each of the four stakeholder groups listed below, identify whether they have high or low interest, and high or low power.

	Interest		Power	
	Low	High	Low	High
Customers				
Government				
Shareholders				
Employees				

68 Kidsplay is a charity that operates a sports centre in a large city.

Kidsplay is managed by a management committee. The committee has decided to build a new, larger sports hall and has started negotiating with three building companies.

The proposed expansion has upset local residents, who are concerned about building site traffic and the danger to their children, and who also believe that the design of the new sports hall is ugly. Three local politicians are members of the residents' committee.

Charity decisions are overseen by a government charity regulator. Historically the regulator has agreed with decisions made by Kidsplay's management committee, except in relation to financial reporting.

Part (i): For each of the following, indicate whether they are internal, connected or external stakeholders.

Stakeholder	Internal	External	Connected
Kidsplay's management committee			
The three building companies			
Local residents			

Part (ii): For each of the stakeholder groups listed below, identify whether they have high or low interest, and high or low power.

	Interest		Power	
	Low	High	Low	High
The three building companies				
Local residents				
The government charity regulator				

69 FCC is a large bank. Which TWO of the following would be classified as connected stakeholders for FCC?

	✓
FCC's shareholders	
FCC's employees	
Customers who borrow money from FCC	
FCC's managers and directors	
The government banking regulator	
The trade union representing FCC's employees	

70 Match the stakeholder with their need/expectation of the company.

Stakeholder	Need/expectation
Government	Pay, working conditions and job security
Shareholders	Dividends and capital growth
Employees	Provision of taxes and jobs and compliance with legislation
Customers	Value-for-money products and services

ORGANISATIONAL STRUCTURE

ORGANISATIONAL STRUCTURE AND GOVERNANCE

71 Which ONE of the following statements regarding the entrepreneurial structure is correct?

	✓
It usually allows for defined career paths for employees	
It often enjoys strong goal congruence throughout the organisation	
It can normally cope with significant diversification and growth	
Control within the organisation tends to be weak	

72 Which ONE of the following is a disadvantage of a functional structure?

	✓
Lack of economies of scale	
Absence of standardisation	
Specialists feel isolated	
Empire building	

73 Which ONE of the following structures is best placed to address the need for co-ordination between different functions in very complex situations?

	✓
Functional	
Divisional	
Matrix	
Geographical	

74 Which ONE of the following structures results in a potential loss of control over key operating decisions and a reduction in goal congruence?

	✓
Matrix	
Entrepreneurial	
Functional	
Geographical	

75 In relation to organisational structures which ONE of the following is the correct definition of the phrase 'span of control'?

	✓
The number of employees that a manager is directly responsible for	
The number of management levels in an organisational structure	
The number of levels in the hierarchy below a given manager	
The number of managers in the organisation	

76 Identify the correct type of structure described by each of the following characteristics.

Characteristic	Entrepreneurial	Functional	Divisional	Matrix
Structured in accordance with product lines or divisions or departments				
Requires dual reporting to managers, for example when a project team member has to report to a project manager as well as a head of their functional department				
Built around the owner manager, who makes all the decisions				
Appropriate for small companies which have few products and locations and which exist in a relatively stable environment				

77 H Ltd makes a variety of unrelated products, including bicycles, furniture and electronics. It is aware that each of these products requires very different strategies and functions. H wishes to use a structure that will allow for each product to be managed separately, but wishes to minimise its overall administrative costs.

Which of the following organisational structures would be most appropriate for H Ltd to adopt?

	✓
Divisional	
Matrix	
Entrepreneurial	
Functional	

78 Which ONE of the following factors would tend to allow an organisation to develop a wide span of control?

	✓
Highly skilled, motivated employees	
Employees spread over a wide geographical area	
Employees undertake complex, changing tasks	

79 Identify whether each of the following statements relating to organisational structure is TRUE or FALSE.

	True	False
A scalar chain refers to the number of levels of management within the organisation.		
Entrepreneurial structures typically suffer from slow decision making.		
An organisation's span of control is unaffected by the nature of the work the organisation undertakes.		

80 Identify whether each of the following statements relating to organisational structure is TRUE or FALSE.

	True	False
Decentralisation tends to reduce training costs within the organisation.		
A matrix structure may increase conflict between managers.		
Tall organisations typically have a narrow span of control.		

81 Identify whether each of the following statements relating to a matrix is TRUE or FALSE.

	True	False
A matrix structure combines the benefits of decentralisation and co-ordination.		
Within a matrix structure, employees will have dual reporting lines.		
A matrix structure is largely theoretical and is rarely used in practice.		
A matrix structure should lead to less duplication across projects and therefore save money.		

82 Consider the following benefits:

(i) Reduced training costs within the organisation

(ii) Better local decisions due to local expertise

(iii) Better motivation of staff

(iv) Reduction in suboptimal behaviour

Which of these are advantages of the centralisation of decision-making within an organisation?

	✓
(i) and (ii) only	
(i), (ii) and (iii) only	
(iii) only	
(i) and (iv) only	

83 The directors of F plc have decided that they need to introduce greater decentralisation within the company.

Which ONE of the following characteristics of F plc would make decentralisation more difficult to implement?

	✓
It has many employees working in various locations	
It operates in many different market sectors	
All managers are very comfortable using modern technologies	
Some senior managers have an authoritative leadership style	

84 The directors of G plc have decided that they need to increase spans of control within the organisation.

Which ONE of the following factors concerning G plc directly limits how many subordinates should report to a single manager?

	✓
The size of the business	
The length of the scalar chain	
Where in the organisational hierarchy the manager is placed	
The extent to which the manager has other responsibilities, such as dealing with customers and suppliers	

THE ROLE OF THE FINANCE FUNCTION

85 Complete the following sentences by placing one of the following options in the spaces.

The preparation of forecasts, for example of future sales or material prices, will be an important role of the finance function _____.

The preparation of comprehensive reports for shareholders will be an important role of the finance function _____.

The preparation of variance analysis for control purposes will be an important role of the finance function _____.

Options:
in narrating how the organisation creates and preserves value
in enabling the organisation to create and preserve value
in shaping how the organisation creates and preserves value

86 Stan is trying to work out how many staff members are going to be required to work on a project next week.

Which role of the finance function best describes what Stan is doing?

	✓
Resource allocation	
Performance management and control	
Planning	
Financial (corporate) reporting	

87 **Which of the following statements is/are true?**

(i) The finance function will help shape how an organisation creates and preserves value through financial (corporate reporting).

(ii) The finance function merely records what has happened over the period in question and as long as it can do that it shouldn't need to be proactive in the way that it is organised.

	✓
Statement (i)	
Statement (ii)	
Both of them	
Neither of them	

88 Which ONE stakeholder of the finance function is most likely to require data on competitors' pricing strategies?

	✓
Sales	
Production	
Shareholders	
Employees	

89 Which ONE stakeholder of the finance function is most likely to require data on employee productivity?

	✓
Production	
Employees	
HR	
Shareholders	

90 Which ONE stakeholder of the finance function is most likely to require data on market trends?

	✓
Employees	
Sales	
Production	
Shareholders	

91 Identify whether each of the following statements relating to the management accounting function is TRUE or FALSE.

	True	False
It is often used by external stakeholders, such as shareholders		
It is a requirement for all limited companies		
It is mainly a historic record of the organisation's activities		
It aids planning and decision making within the business		

92 A toy retailer uses external couriers to deliver any products that are ordered online.

Which ONE of the following KPIs is the best for measuring efficiency in the operations of the toy retailer?

	✓
Percentage on time delivery to customer	
The total level of sales compared to budget	
Percentage on time despatch of goods to customers	
Reorder rate from customers	

93 **Which ONE of the following is an example of co-ordination between the finance function and production?**

	✓
Establishing credit terms	
Advising on prices	
Determining sales quantities	
Budgeting	

94 **Which ONE of the following is a way in which an organisation's marketing department would co-ordinate with its finance function?**

	✓
Calculating charge out rates for services provided by the organisation	
Calculating the budgets for the number of units to be produced	
Estimation of the costs of the raw materials required for production	
Decisions on the quality of raw materials that the organisation can afford to use	

95 E Co has a large marketing department.

In which ONE of the following ways would this department co-ordinate with E's finance function?

	✓
Decisions on the quantity of raw materials required	
Establishing credit terms for customers	
Calculating pay rises for staff	
Decisions on the selling price of the product	

PRACTICE QUESTIONS: SECTION 1

96 G Co is a large manufacturer of mobile phones. G Co also has a number of retail outlets around the world.

Identify which TWO pieces of information G's finance department is likely to receive directly from the HR function rather than from the Operations function.

	✓
Expense claims for production mangers	
Time sheets for production workers	
Overtime rates for production workers	
A production supervisor's retirement date	

RISK

97 Which one of the following sentences best describes risk?

	✓
The exposure to the adverse consequences of dangerous environments.	
The expected impact of uncertain future events on objectives.	
The chance of being caught doing something unethical.	
The impact of the exposure to the adverse consequences of uncertain future events.	

98 Risk management is the process of reducing the adverse consequences either by reducing the _____ of an event or its _____.

What are the two missing words?

	✓
Understanding and impact	
Likelihood and potential	
Understanding and potential	
Likelihood and impact	

99 Match each of the following risks to the appropriate risk category.

Risk category
Business risks
Economic risks
Corporate reputation risks
Political risks

Risk
CEO convicted of illegal share dealing
Disposable income levels fall
Increased regulation of an industry
Raw material prices rise

KAPLAN PUBLISHING

100 Match each of the following risks to the appropriate risk category.

Risk category	Risk
Political risks	Government increases rate of Corporation Tax
Legal risks	Company prosecuted for breach of the Data Protection Act
Regulatory risks	Change of Government
Compliance risks	Customer sues company for negligence

101 The sudden death of the CEO of a small marketing consultancy would best fit which category in a risk map?

	✓
Low probability; low impact	
Low probability; high impact	
High probability; low impact	
High probability; high impact	

102 X is a large retailer, employing over 20,000 sales staff. The retail industry has a reputation for a high level of staff turnover.

The resignation of a member of the sales staff would best fit which category in a risk map?

	✓
Low probability; low impact	
Low probability; high impact	
High probability; low impact	✓
High probability; high impact	

103 The 'TARA' mnemonic is often used to categorise risk management methods. Which one of the following represents the methods in the TARA mnemonic?

	✓
Transfer; Assure; Remove; Accept	
Transfer; Accept; Reduce; Adapt	
Transfer; Avoid; Reduce; Accept	
Transfer; Accept; Remove; Adapt	

104 Metherell Ltd has developed a new cleaning product for use in nuclear reactors. Tests on the product have been successful and the product has been given government approval for use in the UK. However, activist groups claim there is a health risk to humans and wildlife if the product leaks into the water supply. In response to this, the company has taken out an insurance policy to cover any liabilities in the event of a legal claim following a leakage.

Which ONE of the following strategies is Metherell Ltd using to manage its risk exposure?

	✓
Risk avoidance	
Risk reduction	
Risk transfer	
Risk acceptance	

105 BAS is a medium-sized event organiser and is considering how best to manage the risks it faces.

Identify which strategy best describes the following risk management approaches.

	Transfer	Accept	Reduce	Avoid
A race event BAS has organised for next week is an outdoors 5k run. However if it rains it is unlikely to attract enough competitors to make any profit. The management have decided to still hold the event.				
BAS has just taken out a large insurance contract to ensure they are covered if any competitor seeks damages for injuries caused in one of their races.				
One of the employees at BAS has had an innovative idea to hold a waterfall jumping event where competitors compete to jump from the highest possible place along a sheer cliff edge into the North Sea. After considering the idea the BAS management have rejected it as it is too dangerous.				
As part of the organisation of the huge annual showcase event BAS holds, the managers have conducted a large and extensive risk assessment process and put into place all the internal controls they believe to be necessary.				

106 Brantchester Hospital has an excellent record for treating and discharging patients quickly. The hospital is very dependent upon its IT systems to do this, although there have been no significant IT system breakdowns in the last 5 years. Given this, the management team have evaluated the risk due to IT breakdowns as being unlikely ('low probability') but having serious potential implications ('high impact') if anything did go wrong.

Identify which TWO of the following responses to this risk would be most appropriate.

	✓
Keep monitoring the situation	
Accept the risk and continue to operate as normal	
Make sure that good insurance is in place	
Outsource the IT function	
Close departments that would be the most affected by an IT breakdown	

107 OKJ is currently undertaking a risk analysis.

Assess the significance of the risk to OKJ of each of the factors described below.

Factor	Significance
OKJ's home country has recently elected a new government. It is not yet clear if they will introduce new legislation to increase minimum wages. This would have a major impact on OKJ's profitability.	
After a recent accident in one of its factories, OKJ was convicted of breaching relevant health and safety legislation. Based on similar recent cases brought in the industry, OKJ expects to be fined around 7% of its turnover. OKJ has insurance in place that will cover this fine.	
OKJ uses platinum as a key component within some of its products. The price of metals varies significantly on world markets and tends to rise sharply in times of recession. The directors are concerned that its products may become unprofitable if platinum prices rise more than 20% from their current levels, but is uncertain about whether this would happen – even if a recession does occur.	
OKJ is uncertain about whether it can retain its CEO in the long term. It has had a number of CEO's over the last five years – each of them staying very different lengths of time in their roles. Fortunately, OKJ has an experienced Board of Directors and the change in CEOs has had little impact on the business in the past.	

PRACTICE QUESTIONS: SECTION 1

108 Which ONE of the following statements concerning the difference between risk and uncertainty is true?

	✓
The term 'risk' is used when a business only considers potential adverse effects, whereas 'uncertainty' includes looking at potential gains.	
The term 'risk' is used when all possible outcomes can be quantified, whereas 'uncertainty' means future outcomes are unknown.	
The term 'risk' is used when probabilities can be estimated for possible outcomes, whereas 'uncertainty' means we cannot estimate probabilities.	
The term 'risk' is used when probabilities are certain, whereas 'uncertainty' means probabilities are only estimates.	

109 P is a senior manager at a hospital. Currently, eye surgeons perform an average of 3 operations per day and this has left the hospital with a sizeable waiting list for such operations. P wishes to raise this to 5 per day. Surgeons are not being offered a bonus for achieving this new level of performance, but P thinks the surgeons will happily accept the new targets, as it will benefit patients.

P has just announced the new targets to the surgeons, who were annoyed as P had not previously consulted them about this issue. Privately most surgeons have admitted that they could reach 4 operations per day if they hurried through more routine procedures.

Explain TWO potential risks that could arise as a result of the new targets.

1	
2	

110 Q is a local council department, which commissions services from outside contractors to carry out all aspects of the council's work. Q has a list of recommended contractors, many of whom have worked for the council for many years and provide an excellent service at a reasonable price.

Recently, central government announced changes to the health and safety laws in Q's home country. These changes meant that in order to use outside contractors, Q would need to pay for expensive insurance, or insist that contractors apply for a new Health and Safety accreditation certificate. Q does not have a budget to pay for the insurance and to qualify for the certificate contractors must pay for and attend a week long course. As yet, these courses are not available anywhere local to Q.

Central government insists that the new laws will prevent unscrupulous contractors carrying out work without proper safety controls in place. This has been a problem in some areas of the country and led to expensive compensation claims.

Evaluate the following risks to Q arising from the changes to health and safety laws:

Risk	Evaluation
Q's contractor costs may increase.	
Q may no longer be able to use recommended contractors.	
There may be a shortage of contractors for Q to use leading to a backlog of work building up.	
Q may be unable to obtain the relevant insurance.	

EXTERNAL ANALYSIS

PESTLE

111 A cigarette manufacturer is carrying out a PESTLE analysis.

Which THREE of the following factors would be included in this analysis?

	✓
New sources of supply for tobacco	
Government commitments to reduce smoking among young people	
A merger of two rival companies	
A ban on smoking in public places	
An increase in tax on cigarettes	

112 H, a large vehicle manufacturing company in country F, has recently decided to undertake environmental analysis.

Which ONE of the following factors would most likely be identified under the 'social' heading of a PESTLE analysis?

	✓
New CAD and CAM has recently become available for use in F's factories	
Recycling is increasingly important to the residents of country F	
Increased disposable income of consumers within country F	
Changes in minimum wage legislation within country F	

PRACTICE QUESTIONS: SECTION 1

113 Which ONE of the following would a transport company monitor under the 'political' heading as part of a PESTLE analysis?

	✓
Tracking systems to monitor driver hours/anti-theft devices/developments in tyre technology.	
State of the economy/oil price movements/a rise in interest rates.	
Fuel tax/congestion charges in cities/plans to build new roads.	
Predicted car numbers and usage/public concerns over safety.	

114 Consider the following statements:

(1) An aging population represents a risk to all businesses that manufacture or sell technologically advanced products.

(2) Changes in social structure can have a significant impact on a country's buying patterns.

Which of these statements is/are correct?

	✓
(1) only	
(2) only	
Both	
Neither	

115 What change in people's attitudes has put additional pressure on businesses to become more socially responsible?

	✓
Disposable income is growing as people have fewer children.	
More people are living in cities, encouraging companies to build more compact offices.	
Fashion changes rapidly therefore frequently change of suppliers becomes a necessity.	
People are more aware of the 'carbon footprint' left by a company's operations.	

116 Q is a house builder operating in a country where interest rates are at their lowest point for 20 years. The government has been encouraging the building of new houses due to a shortage, particularly of 'affordable housing'. Q has taken full advantage of government schemes to help the population purchase new housing and has invested in new machinery, taken on extra staff and begun to build on many of the sites held in its 'land bank'. Government schemes for buyers include low interest rate government loans and the ability to purchase a share of a home, with the government owning the remaining amount on which rent would be paid according to market rates.

As part of Q's PESTLE analysis, the possibility of interest rate increases has been flagged.

Which TWO of the following are potential consequences for Q of a rise in interest rates?

	✓
Those customers who have purchased houses via government schemes may default on their loans.	
Q may find demand for its new houses decreases.	
Q's own costs may increase.	
The government may withdraw their schemes leading to a drop in demand.	
The cost of land will increase.	

117 Bee Carpets Ltd is a carpet manufacturer based in the UK. The company was founded in the 1920s and has a reputation for high quality carpets, manufactured using natural materials and traditional techniques. This means its cost base is higher than many rivals, mainly due to the higher labour costs involved. However, the carpets command high prices due both to the perceived quality and the choice of selling via prestigious high street retailers.

At the recent board meeting the directors were discussing directions for growth. The Sales Director was keen to develop a new range of cheaper carpets made using fabrics derived from oil products. These could be sold through a wider range of retailers, especially in out-of-town shopping centres, and via a new company website. The CEO was concerned that this could alienate the company's existing, albeit ageing, customer base and suggested these could be marketed under a different brand name to avoid undermining the higher priced products. The Production Director wondered how the cost base could be reduced to support lower prices.

Identify THREE PESTLE categories and, for each category identified, explain how this may have an impact on the future performance of Bee Carpets Ltd, with particular reference to the new range.

PESTLE category	Impact

118 CCC Car Rentals rents out cars in Southern Europe. Founded in 2002, the company has become a leading car rental company in the region, providing a high quality rental service in the premium brand segment. The company gains customers via its sales locations, via its website and mobile app, and though intermediaries. Sales locations are mainly situated at airports and major cities.

The industry saw a major global recession last year and it is now predicted that the industry will not return to previous levels for at least five years and that some car rental companies will not survive. Key trends include the rise in importance and number of online brokers and travel agents, the growth of the low-price value segment, and the use of technology to simplify the customer experience, such as through self-service kiosks, online check-in and automatic rental pick-ups.

For each of the specified PESTLE categories given in the table below, explain TWO possible THREATS to the future performance of CCC Car Rentals, and explain ONE action the company could take to reduce each threat.

PESTLE category	Nature of threat	Action to reduce threat
Economic	1	
	2	
Technological	1	
	2	

119 ZZZ Beds manufactures and sells beds and mattresses in Eastern Europe. The company has a reputation for producing quality products and is now the largest bed and mattress retailer, by revenue, in its home country. The company sells via its 120 owned stores, which are seen as effectively showrooms with knowledgeable, highly trained staff who can address customer needs. All sales are currently limited to just Eastland. Production is highly labour intensive and highly skilled. There is scope for greater automation as the production process is unchanged since 1990.

Sales overall in the market for mattresses and beds are expected to grow by 3.5% p.a., due mainly to an increased awareness of the importance of sleep quality and wellness, and growth in the use of technologies to improve sleep. There is also an increasing awareness of the importance of sustainability, both in terms of the recycling of old mattresses and the choice of materials used in manufacture.

For each of the specified PESTLE categories given in the table below, explain ONE possible THREAT to the future performance of ZZZ Beds, and explain ONE response the company could take to each threat.

PESTLE category	Nature of threat	Response
Technological		
Environmental		

120 Chokolate Box, a listed company, manufactures innovative and accessibly priced luxury chocolate in Southern England. Founded in the 1990s, the company has gained a reputation in the market as a company that produces high quality products and now exports around the world.

Sales growth in the chocolate confectionery industry has been slow over recent years and the industry is expected to continue to grow slowly for the next five years. However, within this, higher growth opportunities exist for organic and dark chocolate products. A major area of concern is an increasing media focus on the health issues surrounding chocolate. The UK Government already has a 'sugar tax' on sugary soft drinks.

For each of the specified PESTLE categories given in the table below, explain ONE possible THREAT to the future performance of Chokolate Box, and explain ONE response the company could take to each threat.

PESTLE category	Nature of threat	Response
Political		
Economic		

THE MICRO-ECONOMIC ENVIRONMENT

121 Which ONE of the following best describes the concept of 'complementary goods'?

	✓
The purchase of one good means that a similar good is not purchased	
A number of goods exist, any of which can be purchased to satisfy a need	
One good is free and the other has to be paid for	
The purchase of one good leads to the purchase of another good	

122 Which ONE of the following will cause the demand curve for a good to shift to the right?

	✓
The price of the good falls	
Disposable income increases	
The supply of the good increases	
The price of a substitute falls	

123 Which ONE of the following will cause the demand curve for a good to shift to the right?

	✓
A reduction in VAT on the materials used to make the good	
An improvement in production which lowers costs	
An increase in the price of the good	
An increase in the supply of a complementary good	

124 Which ONE of the following will NOT cause the supply curve for a good to shift to the right?

	✓
The receipt of a government subsidy	
An increase in employment costs	
Improvements in manufacturing technology	
Lower prices for raw materials	

125 Which ONE of the following would explain a rise in the price of a good accompanied by a fall in the quantity sold?

	✓
The supply curve shifting to the left	
The demand curve shifting to the right	
The demand curve shifting to the left	
The supply curve shifting to the right	

126 The shift to the right in the supply curve on the diagram below can best be explained by which ONE of the following?

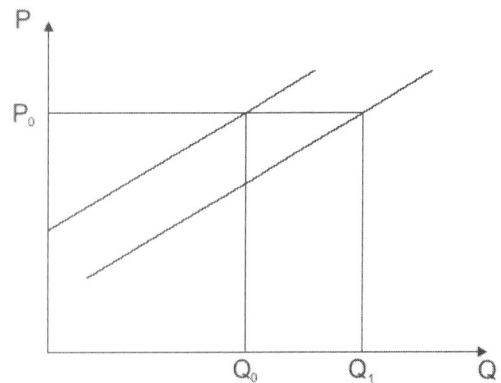

	✓
An increase in the price of the product	
An increase in the price of raw materials	
A rise in the amount of wages paid to labour	
The result of technological progress	

127 In the diagram below, what action will suppliers take at the price of P_{high}?

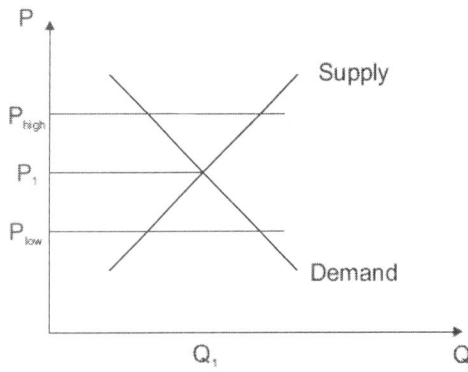

	✓
Increase supply to take advantage of the high price	
Supply the same quantity of goods but at a reduced price	
Supply a reduced quantity of goods but at the same price	
Decrease price to attract more demand, and reduce excess supply	

128 Which ONE of the following best describes the concept of 'substitute goods'?

	✓
The purchase of one good means that a similar good is not purchased	
A competitor providing the same good	
One good is free and the other has to be paid for	
The purchase of one good leads to the purchase of another good	

129 Which of the following is NOT held constant when we draw a demand curve?

	✓
The price of complementary goods	
The price of substitutes	
Consumers' income	
The price of the good	

130 A demand curve is drawn assuming all but one of the following remains unchanged. Which ONE item can vary?

	✓
Consumer tastes	
The price of the product	
The price of other products	
Disposable income	

131 Which ONE of the following statements best describes the movement from P_0 to P_1 in the diagram below?

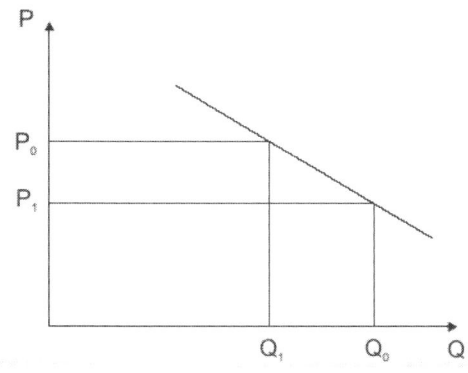

	✓
An outward shift in the demand curve	
A fall in the supply of the good	
An expansion along the demand curve	
A fall in demand	

AAT: BUSINESS AWARENESS

132 In the diagram below the equilibrium price for chocolate is P_0 and Q_0.

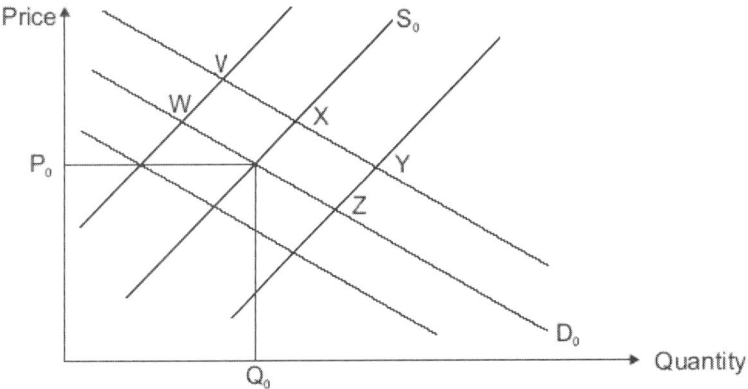

What will the new equilibrium price be if there is an increase in the price of cocoa beans (an ingredient in chocolate)?

	✓
V	
W	
X	
Y	
Z	

SUSTAINABILITY

133 Which of the following would best explain the concept of sustainable development?

	✓
Starting business in the developed countries where the economic climate is conducive to trade.	
Development which meets the needs of the present without compromising the ability of future generations to meet their own needs.	
Sustaining the production at the level of maximum capacity.	
Developing the business by signing long-term contracts with suppliers.	

134 HGF Ltd is considering implementing a corporate social responsibility (CSR) policy. However it is concerned that there may be drawbacks to this.

Which TWO of the following are possible problems caused by a CSR policy?

	✓
Increased materials cost	
Failure to attract and retain quality employees	
Loss of management time	
Loss of key business skills	

PRACTICE QUESTIONS: SECTION 1

135 A Ltd is considering improving its impact on the environment by adopting a sustainable approach to business.

Identify whether each of the following statements relating to A's decision is TRUE or FALSE.

	True	False
It may help to reduce the organisation's operating costs		
It could lead to an improved relationship with shareholders and other stakeholders		
It may improve employee motivation		
It would be expected to reduce the administrative burden on management		

136 Choke Ltd purchases a number of raw materials from various suppliers and uses them to create material G. This material takes a long time to degrade in the environment and poses a risk to animal and plant life for several decades. Any stocks of G that have been unsold for more than one month are no longer saleable and have to be disposed of.

Which ONE of the following would be most helpful to Choke in minimising the impact that wastage of material G has on the environment?

	✓
Sourcing raw materials from environmentally friendly suppliers	
Improved communication with customers to identify likely demand	
Improved energy efficiency of the production process for material G	
Reduction in packaging on the units of material G that are sold	

137 Identify the correct type of sustainability that each of the following policies relates to.

Policy	Social sustainability	Environmental sustainability	Financial sustainability
A Ltd aims to be carbon neutral across all of its operations within 3 years.			
B Ltd has detailed financial and non-financial targets to ensure it can achieve its strategic plans to grow shareholder wealth.			
C Ltd offers all employees opportunities for advancement, training and CPD.			

138 Which of the following is NOT a way in which businesses can reduce the amount of damage they cause to the environment?

	✓
Rebranding of products	
Recycling	
Redesigning products to use fewer materials	
Careful production planning	

139 Recycling waste material could be classed as being both environmentally friendly AND sustainable.

Is this statement TRUE or FALSE?

	✓
True	
False	

140 Which of the following statements best describes 'corporate social responsibility'?

	✓
A company should play an active part in the social life of the local neighbourhood.	
A company should be sensitive to the needs of all stakeholders.	
A company should be alert to the social needs of all employees.	
A company should act responsibly in relation to shareholders' overall needs – not just their financial needs.	

141 Identify whether each of the following statements relating to sustainability is TRUE or FALSE.

	True	False
Sustainability involves taking a long-term view and allowing the needs of present generations to be met without compromising the ability of future generations to meet their own needs.		
Sustainability involves considering the needs of the organisation's shareholders only.		
Accountants have a public interest duty to protect society as a whole and the organisation's sustainability.		

142 MLC is a clothing retailer who imports clothes from diverse suppliers worldwide. MLC has a very strong, well-publicised corporate ethical code. The company accountant has just found out that one of MLC suppliers use child labour in the manufacture of their clothes and pay very low wages with cramped, dangerous conditions. This is in breach of contract conditions with that supplier.

Which ONE of the following statements best describes the actions MLC should take in the light of this?

	✓
Place more orders with the supplier – its cheap labour so the margins are good, which should keep the shareholders happy.	
Leave things as they are and hope the information doesn't get out.	
Continue trading with the supplier but investigate the claims quietly.	
Cancel all contracts with the supplier and release a press statement stating how the company will always act quickly and decisively if unethical practices are suspected.	

143 **Which THREE of the following are common arguments FOR organisations adopting a strong commitment to sustainability?**

	✓
Increased profitability due to cost reductions	
Faster strategic decision-making	
Improved reputation with environmentally conscious customers	
Ability to attract higher calibre staff	
Reduced risk of government intervention in the future	

144 Tio Rino is a global mining company that has received much criticism in the past over its sustainability record. Press coverage has focussed on environmental damage, pollution, labour and human rights abuses and deforestation as well as criticism that Tio Rino mines coal (which contributes to global warming when burnt) and uranium (which contributes to concerns over nuclear power).

However, on its website the firm states the following:

'Our business is sustainably finding, mining and processing mineral resources.'

FOR EACH of the Triple Bottom Line reporting headings suggest TWO ways that a mining company such as Tio Rino can be a sustainable mining company.

People

Profit

Planet

ETHICS

ETHICS

145 N, a member in practice, has been tasked to complete an important assignment. However, they know that they will not have enough time complete the work properly.

Indicate which fundamental ethical principle is under threat. Select ONE answer only.

	✓
Integrity	
Confidentiality	
Professional competence and due care	
Professional behaviour	
Objectivity	

146 Bella, a professional accountant, was invited on a 'night out' with others from the accounts department. This became quite a boisterous evening and it ended with the Finance Director removing a sign from the front of a shop which they brought into the office the next day as a reminder of the good evening.

(i) **Indicate which fundamental ethical principle is under threat. Select ONE answer only.**

	✓
Integrity	
Confidentiality	
Professional competence and due care	
Professional behaviour	
Objectivity	

(ii) **Indicate what course of action Bella should take.**

	✓
Do nothing – a sign is not worth losing your job over	
Suggest to the FD that they should replace the sign	

147 Your boss has told you that there are going to be some redundancies in the company. You will not be affected, but your boss has named a number of people who will be, including a good friend of yours, L, who is in the process of buying a holiday home in Cornwall. You know that your friend would not be able to afford the property if they were to lose their job and that they would pull out of the purchase if they knew about the redundancy plans.

The news of the redundancies will not be made public for several weeks.

(i) **Indicate which fundamental ethical principle is under threat. Select ONE answer only.**

	✓
Integrity	
Confidentiality	
Professional competence and due care	
Professional behaviour	
Objectivity	

(ii) Indicate your best course of action

	✓
From an ethical point of view you should tell your friend about the redundancies on the grounds it could save them unnecessary financial problems and distress.	
You should not tell your friend about the redundancies.	

148 You are a management accountant working a UK listed chemical company. During the course of your duties, you become aware that the company is dumping waste illegally. You have raised this with your manager who has told you to ignore the issue.

Which ONE of the following is NOT an appropriate course of action to take next?

	✓
Contacting AAT's ethical helpline for advice	
Reporting the company to the environment agency	
Contacting a journalist at a national newspaper	
Taking the matter to the Audit committee	

149 Alessandro is an AAT member in practice employed by Sueka LLP, and has acquired some information about Polina Ltd in the course of acting for the company on an assurance engagement. Complete the following sentence by selecting the appropriate option from the three options given below.

'The principle of confidentiality imposes an obligation on Alessandro to refrain from which ONE of the following?

	✓
using the information to the advantage of Sueka LLP'	
disclosing the information within Sueka LLP'	
disclosing the information to anyone at Polina Ltd'	

150 V, a member in practice, performs book-keeping services for both Yen Ltd and Piston Ltd. The two companies are in dispute about a series of purchases that Yen Ltd made from Piston Ltd.

Indicate which TWO fundamental ethical principles are under threat.

	✓
Integrity	
Confidentiality	
Professional competence and due care	
Professional behaviour	
Objectivity	

PRACTICE QUESTIONS: **SECTION 1**

151 S is a professional accountant working in practice.

Kept Ltd is S's oldest client and as well as the usual accountancy and tax services, S has recently been asked to write a reference to a new landlord confirming that Kept Ltd is likely to be able to pay its rent for the next 3 years.

While this would normally not be a problem, S is aware that Kept Ltd has been experiencing financial difficulties over the last 6 months, so S is wary of writing such a reference. To offer some reassurance, the Chief accountant has offered to pay S a large fee for supplying the reference and suggested S should include a disclaimer of liability.

Analyse S's dilemma from an ethical point of view.

152 Cosby plc owns a small chain of supermarkets with an emphasis on organic, local produce. The Directors of Cosby plc are concerned that, despite having better quality produce than rivals, it is not competing as well as it would like against national supermarket chains.

The Marketing Director, Manu has proposed that Cosby plc should set up a new corporate code of ethics that could be used as part of its marketing effort. They are convinced that many customers will be influenced by such a code and has suggested that the following aspects could be incorporated:

1   All products should be purchased from local farms and suppliers where appropriate.

2   All packing materials should be obtained from renewable sources where feasible.

3   All suppliers to be paid on time.

4   All suppliers to be paid fair prices as determined by the Purchasing Manager.

Comment on EACH of the ethical values suggested by the Marketing Director, highlighting the benefit of each, together with any reservations you may have concerning them.

1   All products should be purchased from local farms and suppliers where appropriate.

2	All packing materials should be obtained from renewable sources where feasible.
3	All suppliers to be paid on time.
4	All suppliers to be paid fair prices as determined by the Purchasing Manager.

153 J, an AAT member in practice, is conducting a second interview of A, an excellent candidate (also an AAT member), for a senior post in J's firm. When discussing remuneration A states they will bring a copy of the database of clients from their old firm to introduce new clients to J's firm. A also says they know a lot of negative information about their old firm which J could use to gain clients from them.

Identify which of the following are the most appropriate actions for J to take following the interview.

	Appropriate	Not appropriate
Because A shows business acumen, offer them the job.		
Because A has breached the fundamental principles of integrity and confidentiality, report them to the AAT.		
Because A lacks integrity, inform them that they will not be offered the job.		

154 J is an AAT member in practice at Khan LLP. They are a senior on an assurance assignment for Brittle plc. They inherit a 10% shareholding in this client.

(i) Identify which type of threat this situation represents.

	✓
Self-interest threat	
Self-review threat	
Intimidation threat	
Advocacy threat	
Familiarity threat	

(ii) Identify what J's best course of action would be.

	✓
Continue as senior but make the partners aware of the inheritance	
Ask to be removed from the assignment	
Resign from Khan LLP	
Report the matter to the National Crime Agency (NCA)	

155 Suresh has audited the accounts of Believe It plc as part of the assurance team for the past five years. Suresh has been approached by Believe It plc with an offer of the Senior Accountant role.

(i) Identify which type of threat this situation represents.

	✓
Self-interest threat	
Self-review threat	
Intimidation threat	
Advocacy threat	
Familiarity threat	

(ii) **Suggest TWO safeguards the assurance firm should have in place concerning such a threat.**

1
2

156 G is an AAT member working for Kutchins Ltd, an engineering consultancy. G has recently started this job, having previously worked for an accountancy firm where they were the audit senior for Kirk Ltd, a competitor of Kutchins Ltd.

Explain whether G is allowed to use knowledge, information and experience gained from their previous employer in their new job.

MONEY LAUNDERING

157 Connor, a member in practice, has just received a call from a potential new client asking for help in relation to a business transaction. However when asked for the address, the client said they would rather not say.

Identify which of the following are the most appropriate actions for Connor to take.

	Appropriate	Not appropriate
Continue with forging a relationship with the client in the usual manner.		
Inform the client that without knowing the correct address the client/accountant relationship cannot be forged.		
Consider reporting the conversation to the National Crime Agency (NCA).		

158 J, a member in practice has recently come across what they believe is an investigation by the regulatory authorities into allegations of money laundering at a large client.

(i) J decides to communicate this to the Finance Director of the client. What offence J will commit if they do this?

	✓
Breach of confidentiality	
Tipping off	
Money laundering	

(ii) What is the maximum sentence that J can receive if found guilty of the offence?

	✓
2 years	
5 years	
10 years	
14 years	

(iii) J's defence includes the claim that their organisation does not have a MLRO (Money Laundering Reporting Officer). In the absence of an MLRO, who should J have approached with their concerns?

	✓
HMRC	
The National Crime Agency (NCA)	
The national press	

159 T, an accountant in practice, has recently been working on the tax computations for a client, Stoppard plc. In preparing this year's tax returns T realised that they made an error preparing the last tax returns which resulted in an underpayment. T told the Finance Director of Stoppard plc about the error but the Finance Director is refusing to tell the HMRC, claiming 'T made the mistake, not me'.

Identify whether each of the following statements is TRUE or FALSE.

	True	False
Funds retained after discovery of a tax error amount to money laundering by Stoppard plc.		
T should report the matter to the National Crime Agency (NCA).		
T needs to make an authorised disclosure to the National Crime Agency NCA.		

160 Rani, an AAT member within the UK, works for a firm of accountants, LOFT and Co, with a range of clients. LOFT and Co recently billed a client, H Ltd, £5,000 and were very surprised when they received a cheque for £50,000 in settlement of the invoice. The Finance Director of H Ltd explained to Rani that it was a mistake on their part but asked whether LOFT and Co could send a cheque for the overpayment of £45,000 to Q Ltd, a different company and not one of LOFT's clients.

Discuss whether or not LOFT and Co should agree to the payment.

161 Meera works for a large accountancy firm as a tax specialist. Recently two matters have arisen:

Matter 1

On Monday Meera was in a meeting with a potential new client.

The potential client started by stating that they felt Meera's fees proposal was far too high and Meera needed to reduce the fee substantially.

The client then said that they believed their tax bill for the previous year was also too high but if Meera guaranteed to reduce this tax bill, then they would come to Meera's firm.

Meera has had a quick look at the figures and believes the sum looked reasonable.

(a) **Explain what Meera should do in response to the client's requests.**

Matter 2

On Tuesday Meera had a dispute with Greg, a new client. After analysing Greg's tax affairs Meera had found a material error in the previous year's tax return that resulted in an underpayment of tax. The previous tax computations were prepared by Greg's previous accountant.

Meera advised Greg to tell HMRC about the error but so far Greg has refused to do so, claiming it is 'their problem, not mine'.

(b) Should Meera tell HRMC about the error?

(c) What should Meera do if Greg continues to refuse to inform the HMRC?

162 K is involved in illegal activities, from which they make a considerable amount of money. In order to conceal these gains from the illegal activities, K bought a bookshop intending to pass off the illegally gained money as profits from the legitimate bookshop business.

K employs L to act as the manager of the bookshop and M as the accountant to produce false business accounts for the bookshop business.

(a) Explain what is meant by money laundering, the different categories of offence and possible punishments.

(b) Analyse the above scenario from the perspective of the law relating to money laundering. In particular, explain which criminal offences may have been committed by the various parties.

TECHNOLOGY AFFECTING BUSINESS

TECHNOLOGY

163 How is the delivery of on-demand computing resources otherwise known?

	✓
Artificial Intelligence	
The Internet of things	
Big data	
Cloud computing	

164 The process by which users log on to remote servers to access and process their files is best known as what?

	✓
Cloud computing	
Wide Area Network	
The internet	
Remote working	

PRACTICE QUESTIONS: SECTION 1

165 What are the TWO main types of cloud computing?

	✓
Public Cloud	
Restricted Cloud	
Private Cloud	
Amazon Cloud	

166 Which THREE of the following are disadvantages of cloud computing?

	✓
Scalability	
Contract management	
Potential job losses	
Reliance on a third party	
Increases cost	
Reduced flexibility for employees	

167 Which THREE of the following are advantages of cloud computing?

	✓
Cost efficiency	
Scalability	
Flexibility	
Contract management	
Career opportunities	
Highlights inefficiencies	

168 Which ONE of the following statements is true?

	✓
Process automation is only feasible for simple, repetitive tasks	
Process automation in complex business areas is beyond the limits of technology	
Process automation can enable a business to save costs	
Process automation usually leads to employee dissatisfaction	

169 Machines working and reacting like human beings describes what?

	✓
Robotics	
Voice recognition	
Artificial intelligence	
The 4th Industrial Revolution	

170 Which of the following is a definition of a blockchain?

	✓
A technology that allows people who do not know each other to trust a shared record of events.	
A centralised, undistributed and private digital ledger that is used to record transactions.	
A sequence of transactions facilitated by the internet.	
A supply chain management system used to improve efficiency.	

171 Which THREE of the following statements about a blockchain are true?

	✓
Blockchain is regarded as a solution to cyber security risk	
Records in the blockchain are publically available and distributed across everyone that is part of the network of participants	
Records in the blockchain are always kept private to enhance security	
The verification of transactions is carried out by computers	
The verification of transaction is carried out by individuals	

172 What is the internet of things?

	✓
An interactive collection of websites enabling users to communicate with one another.	
A technology that allows people who do not know each other to trust a shared record of event.	
Smart phones that enable users to control appliances within their home such as their heating or lighting.	
A network of smart devices with inbuilt software and connectivity which connect to the internet.	

173 Advancements in mobile technology have contributed to the decline in the newspaper industry?

Is this statement true or false?

	✓
True	
False	

174 Which THREE of the following are consequences of the developments in mobile technologies?

	✓
The decline of the newspaper industry	
The decline of social media interactions	
The decline in the number of retail bank branches	
An increase in the on demand nature of music	
An increase in the cost to manufacture smart devices	

175 TPO Company manufactures jewellery and has been looking at ways to improve its customers' experience. It has decided to enable customers to customise their purchases. The company's first goal is to identify the preferences of its different customer groups.

Which ONE of the following tools will most help TPO achieve this goal?

	✓
Artificial intelligence	
Data analytics	
Process automation	
Data visualisation	

176 Which of the following is a disadvantage of cloud computing?

	✓
Increased flexibility to working arrangements	
More reliance on third party suppliers	
Access to continually up to date software	
Easier integration of systems	

177 Cloud computing enables multiple users to collaborate on a file at the same time, although this increases the risk of version control issues.

Is this statement true or false?

	✓
True	
False	

178 Which THREE of the following are advantages of investing in process automation within the finance function?

	✓
Staff time can be freed up to focus on value adding activities	
No extra training will be required for staff as they will no longer be processing manually	
Staff will automatically buy in to having the mundane work taken from them	
Headcount reductions	
Improved efficiency	

179 Which of the following statements regarding blockchain are true?

(i) Blockchain technology involves the use of a distributed ledger.

(ii) Cryptocurrencies should be considered as intangible assets in the financial statements.

(iii) The use of blockchain technologies removes the need for traditional intermediaries in transactions.

(iv) Blockchain solutions will not overcome the issue of slow cross border payments.

	✓
(i) and (ii)	
(i) and (iii)	
(iii) and (iv)	
(i), (ii) and (iii)	

PRACTICE QUESTIONS: SECTION 1

180 So Handy is a relatively young business comprising a franchised network of labourers such as plumbers, electricians and carpenters. Each franchisee has an app that enables them to log and record the expenses they incur as well as scanning all receipts for materials purchased.

What type of technology are they making use of?

	✓
Social media	
Internet of things	
An intranet	
Mobile technology	

DATA PROTECTION

181 Identify whether each of the following statements concerning principles within GDPR is TRUE or FALSE.

	True	False
Data must not be kept for longer than five years		
Data must be used for a specified, explicit purpose		
Data held must be accurate		
Data must be used transparently		
Data should always be in a hard copy format		

182 Compliance with GDPR is the only thing that matters where data usage is concerned.

Is this statement TRUE or FALSE?

	✓
True	
False	

183 Data Protection legislation, such as The Data Protection Act in the UK, typically focuses on which ONE of the following?

	✓
Issues concerning data held about incorporated entities	
Rights of the individual with regards to withholding information about oneself	
The way data about the individual is to be obtained, used and stored	
Aligning the information requirements between different countries	

184 Which of the following are typical rights of individuals with respect to data stored about them in data protection legislation?

	Yes	No
Right of subject access – individuals are entitled to be told whether the data controller holds personal data about them.		
Right to prevent processing for the purposes of direct marketing.		

185 Consider the following two scenarios.

(i) Annan wants to request their personal credit report from a credit file company for free, using typical data protection legislation.

(ii) Annan receives a large amount of unsolicited (junk) mail. Using the data protection act, Annan wishes to have these marketing activities blocked.

In which of these scenarios would typical data protection legislation support Annan?

	✓
(i) only	
(ii) only	
Both	
Neither	

INFORMATION-SECURITY AND CYBER-SECURITY

186 The Senior Finance Manager at H Ltd received an email that appeared to be from BST, H's bank. The email asked for the manager to confirm some of the security in formation, by clicking on a link and answering some questions. At the end of the week, one of the manager's direct reports flagged some unusual transactions while carrying out routine bank reconciliations. There were several large payments to unknown sources.

Which ONE of the following cyber-attacks does it appear that H Ltd was a victim of?

	✓
Keylogging	
Screenshotting	
Phishing	
Distributed denial of service	

PRACTICE QUESTIONS: SECTION 1

187 Which type of cyber-attack involves criminals recording what a user types onto they keyboard?

	✓
Phishing	
Keylogging	
File hijacking	
Denial of service	

188 Jenny Green, the financial controller of ABC Ltd, recently received an email that appeared to be from the company's bank. It instructed Jenny to click on a link and confirm some of the company's security information. Just days later, Jenny noticed that money had been taken unexpectedly out of ABC Ltd's bank account.

Which ONE of the following cyber-attacks does it appear that ABC Ltd was a victim of?

	✓
Phishing	
Keylogging	
File Hijacking	
Denial of service	

189 The board of GJH Company have approved a number of proposals to be completed in the next period.

Which THREE of the following proposals would have an impact on the company's cyber-security risk?

	✓
Changing the specification of their best-selling product	
Acquiring a new manufacturing facility	
Revaluing non-current assets	
Outsourcing the Human Resources department	
Replacing laptops used by the sales force	

AAT: BUSINESS AWARENESS

190 FFK Company is a small manufacturing company supplying wholesale customers who order goods by phone. It operates from one site and has its own internal accounts department. Labels for goods to be despatched are printed on-site and the goods are then collected by a local courier service for delivery. Inventory levels for key components are monitored electronically and suppliers receive automatic notification when deliveries are required.

Based on the information provided, which ONE of the following features of FFK Company's business model is MOST likely to expose them to cyber-security threats?

	✓
Orders placed by phone	
Internal accounts department	
Use of a local courier service	
Inventory arrangement with component suppliers	

191 For each of the following scenarios, comment on whether it would impact cyber-security risk:

Scenario	Comment
A business acquires a competitor.	
A large training organisation changes its organisational structure from divisional based on geography to a matrix structure.	
A local market trader who usually works Monday to Friday decides to open a stall at a new Sunday market.	
A window cleaning business changes from accepting cash only to allowing customer to pay online.	

192 Which TWO of the following would NOT be recommended to a business to help reduce cyber risks?

	✓
Regular IT training for staff	
Implementing access controls	
Ensure all staff to use the same memorable password so that people don't forget it	
Keeping software security up to date	
Establish and communicate IT policies and procedures	
Allowing all staff the freedom to use social media without any limitations to help motivate them	

193 For each of the following statements, identify whether they should be included in an IT policy document advising on password security.

Statement	Included?
Use the same passwords for work and personal accounts, to make it easier for you to remember it	
When the IT department ask for your password to work on your PC you must always give it to them	
Keep a list of all your passwords either in your desk or another convenient location in case you forget them	
Create strong passwords that are difficult to guess	
Password321 is a stronger password than S9v£E1X	

194 BUS Ltd is a training organisation and the board is becoming increasingly concerned about cyber threats. The IT manager has proposed that the organisation should ban the use of USB drives on work computers. The board is reluctant to sanction this because the use of USB drives is widespread by their employees and they feel it will meet with significant resistance.

Identify whether each of the following statements given by the IT manager about why USB devices should be banned is TRUE or FALSE.

	True	False
USB drives could contain malware and, when inserted into a network device, the malware could infect BUS Ltd systems.		
Sensitive information could be stolen from BUS Ltd by employees using USB drives.		
There are no controls that could protect sensitive information from being stolen on a USB drive.		
Antivirus software may not be able to prevent malware from a USB drive.		
Employees losing USB drives containing sensitive information also presents a cyber-risk to BUS Ltd.		

195 F&T Co is a small family owned business making sandwiches and cakes for sale in their local region. The company has a head office, a small factory and two shops. The four sites while in fairly close proximity are all linked by the company's computer systems to help efficient stock control. This is important as their produce is perishable and they need to avoid wastage. As they have a small seating area in each shop, the two shops offer free customer Wi-Fi.

The small board of F&T is meeting to discuss the cyber risks they face.

Identify whether each of the following statements that were made at the meeting is TRUE or FALSE.

	True	False
Now our staff have been trained on email use and phishing, F&T Co will be protected from cyber-attacks as long as our staff do not open emails from senders they do not recognise		
We only need to worry about external threats to our IT systems		
The new antivirus software that we installed should help prevent our systems from being attacked		
Paying someone to monitor the data moving across our network is a waste of resources and time		

196 XYZ plc, a large online retailer, recently suffered a cyber-attack that resulted in the company website crashing due to being overwhelmed with vast amounts of traffic.

Which ONE of the following cyber-attacks does it appear that XYZ plc was a victim of?

	✓
Keylogging	
File hijacking	
Phishing	
Distributed denial of service	

INFORMATION AND BIG DATA

197 J has been asked to collect some information for their manager. It takes J 14 hours to gather the information and when it was presented to the manager it was immediately filed away.

Which of the characteristics of good quality information is NOT being exhibited?

	✓
Understandable	
Complete	
Cost < benefit	
Accurate	

PRACTICE QUESTIONS: SECTION 1

198 In the context of data gathering and quality, which of the following statements are true?

(i) The technology available merely takes the legwork out of data gathering, everything that is available now was available in the past, but it was too time consuming to gather it.

(ii) With the improved data comes with it the need to be able to respond quickly. Shorter lead times are an essential aspect of improved data.

	✓
(i) only	
(ii) only	
Both are true	
Neither are true	

199 How are medium-term decisions better known?

	✓
Strategic	
Managerial	
Operational	
Tactical	

200 B is in discussion with some colleagues (at the same level of the organisational hierarchy) about which, if any, acquisitions to make using the surplus funds of the business. They are choosing between two similar businesses.

Which level of decision-making are they engaging in?

	✓
Strategic	
Tactical	
Acquisitional	
Operational	

201 Connecting machines on the internet of things to collect real time data has many advantages for a manufacturing business.

Monitoring the performance of the machines enables which ONE of the following advantages specifically?

	✓
Forecasting	
Preventative maintenance	
Improved service for customers	
Supply chain collaboration	

AAT: BUSINESS AWARENESS

202 Which THREE of the following statements relating to big data are true?

	✓
Big data refers to any financial data over $1 billion	
The defining characteristics of big data are velocity, volume and variety	
Managing big data effectively can lead to increased competitive advantage	
The term big data means 'data that comes from many sources'	
Big data contains both financial and non-financial data	

203 Assessing the reliability of big data refers to which of the 5 Vs?

	✓
Value	
Velocity	
Volume	
Visibility	
Veracity	

204 Which of the 5 Vs of big data refers to the constant stream of data being produced?

	✓
Value	
Variety	
Veracity	
Volume	
Velocity	

205 The need for systems to validate data links to which of the 5 Vs of big data?

	✓
Value	
Variety	
Veracity	
Volume	
Velocity	

PRACTICE QUESTIONS: SECTION 1

206 In the world of big data and the role of accountants, which of the following statements are true?

(i) Although there is more data, the basic analysis techniques used should be the same and so no upskilling is needed.

(ii) Experts may be needed to provide additional analysis of the data.

	✓
(i) only	
(ii) only	
Both are true	
Neither are true	

207 FGH plc is a large fashion clothing retailer with stores in many countries, both on traditional high streets and in out-of-town shopping centres. FHG also has a significant online presence and has seen major growth in website sales. FGH introduced a loyalty card five years ago that enables customers to earn vouchers, gain discounted prices in-store and get priority access to sales events. Approximately 60% of regular customers now have loyalty cards. FGH also asks card holders to complete regular surveys concerning customer satisfaction, future buying intentions, preferred sales channels and so on.

(a) Identify the big data characteristic that matches each statement below.

Statement	Volume	Velocity	Variety	Veracity
FGH collects data from tens of thousands of customers each day, whether in stores or when logged into the website.				
FGH compares data from different stores in order to assess whether or not identified trends are reliable.				
FGH uses extensive AI within a comprehensive data analytics system to analyse data obtained from loyalty cards in real time.				
FGH collects data from all stores, of each type, from each country and from each customer type.				

(b) Identify whether the following statements are TRUE or FALSE.

	True	False
Survey responses will be fully representative of customer attitudes and behaviours.		
Survey responses will be difficult to analyse due to the volume of data generated.		
Survey responses will be too detailed to be of any use for making strategic decisions.		

208 S has recently started looking at ways of gathering big data for their business. S is concerned that some of the sources of data they have chosen are unreliable and may therefore lead them to inaccurate conclusions.

Which characteristic of Big Data may be missing from S's data?

	✓
Value	
Variety	
Veracity	
Volume	
Velocity	

209 CCC Health Trust is a large healthcare provider with 25 hospitals and other facilities within its control. The Trust collects and analyses a wide range of data, including the following:

- patients – vital signs, medication administered, time spent with medical staff, time spent in the hospital, food and drink, medical history, consultants' notes, outcomes (e.g. whether an operation was a success), and satisfaction survey feedback
- staff – hours worked, shift patterns, activities (e.g. surgery).

Identify whether the following statements are TRUE or FALSE.

	True	False
Use of Big Data can reduce costs.		
Use of Big Data can reduce waiting times.		
The use of Big Data in healthcare poses new ethical and legal challenges.		

COMMUNICATING INFORMATION

VISUALISING AND COMMUNICATING INFORMATION

210 **The use of a dashboard to present data is an example of what?**

	✓
Data visualisation	
Data simplification	
Graphical data	
Information processing	

211 The provision of information in a more appealing and understandable manner is often referred to as what?

	✓
Artificial Intelligence	
Data simplification	
Cloud computing	
Data visualisation	

212 Which of the following is NOT necessarily a benefit of data visualisation?

	✓
Improves the accuracy of the data being analysed	
Problem areas can be identified sooner	
Understandable by many users	
Supports prompt decision making	

213 Which ONE of the following statements about data visualisation is true?

	✓
The most common use of data visualisation is the creation of a dashboard displaying real time KPIs.	
Data is always displayed in standardised formats to ensure consistency.	
Data visualisation refers to data that is analysed using virtual reality software.	
Increased use of data visualisation within organisations increases the need for more IT experts.	

214 ELC Co has produced some infographics to enable the visualisation of its sales data.

Which THREE of the following characteristics will make the infographics more effective?

	✓
Details of sales made to each customer on a daily basis	
The ability to drill down to obtain further detail	
Avoidance of technical jargon	
Access granted to all sales staff	
Intuitive visualisations needing little explanation	

215 Directors will be the stakeholder of the finance function most likely to require data visualisation.

Is this statement true or false?

	✓
True	
False	

216 Non-financial managers are likely to experience problems in understanding and interpreting management accounting reports.

Which ONE of the following statements is the least appropriate method of dealing with this problem?

	✓
Highlight and explain any unusual items in the report	
Discuss with users the most appropriate form of report	
Include clear graphics and charts, and ensure that the narrative is as simple as possible	
Ensure that only individuals with some accounting knowledge are appointed to management positions	
Highlight and explain any unusual items in the report	

217 A company manufactures three products and wants to show how sales of each product have changed from 20X1 to 20X8, whilst also analysing the change in total sales.

Which ONE of the following charts or diagrams would be most suitable for showing this information?

	✓
Pie chart	
Component bar chart	
Simple bar chart	
Multiple bar chart	

218 XYZ produces three main products. Which would be the most appropriate chart or diagram for showing total turnover and its product analysis month by month?

	✓
Area chart	
Line graph	
Pie chart	
Component bar chart	

219 What would be the most effective way of demonstrating a trend in new mobile telephone sales from January to December 20X1?

	✓
Pie chart	
Bar chart	
Table	
Line graph	

220 Which ONE of the following graphs would best be used to provide exact data?

	✓
Pie chart	
Bar chart	
Table	
Line graph	

221 Which member of the sales team had the highest sales in February?

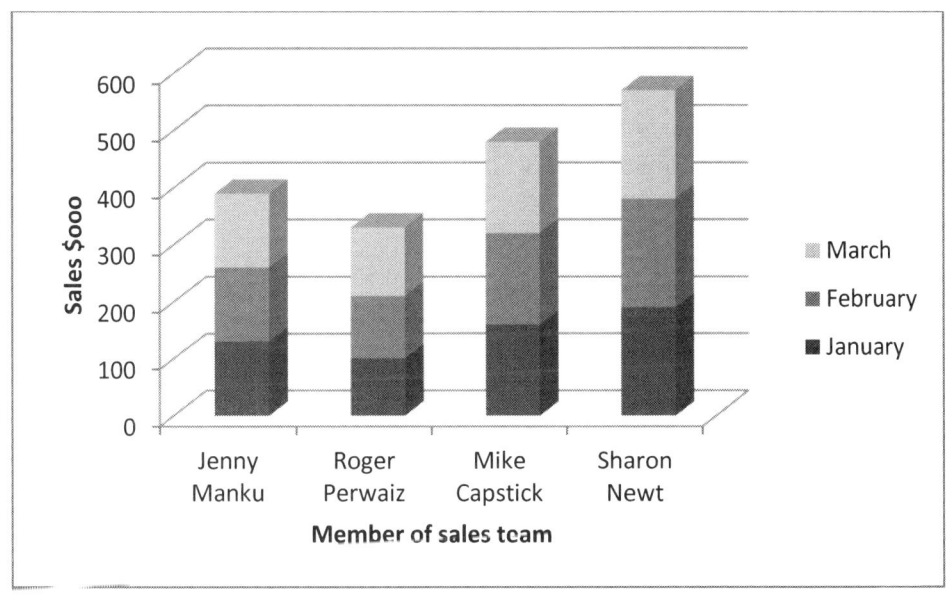

	✓
Jenny Manku	
Roger Perwaiz	
Mike Capstick	
Sharon Newt	

222 Referring to the graph which statements are true and which are false?

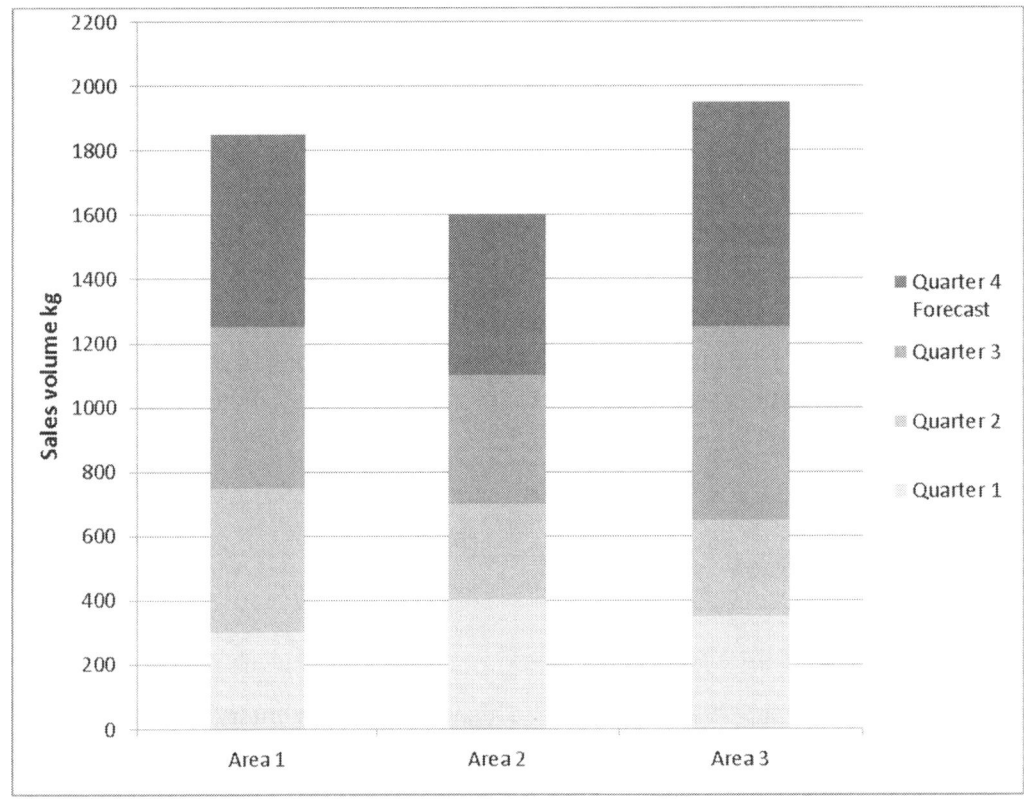

	True	False
Area 3 shows the best performance in Q3		
Area 2 sales are consistent quarter on quarter		
Q4 has the largest volume of sales across all areas		
Area 1 shows the best performance in Q2		

223 Many companies now present key data, such as that relating to sales performance, in dashboards with a range of visualisations, charts and diagrams.

Explain the benefits of such dashboards.

224 Higgs and Co make and sell chocolate animals. These are sold through a range of retail outlets. The company is always keen to find new outlets and were very pleased to win a contract with a major supermarket chain in April. It is now July.

The following represents part of a performance dashboard for a chocolate unicorn that was introduced in January:

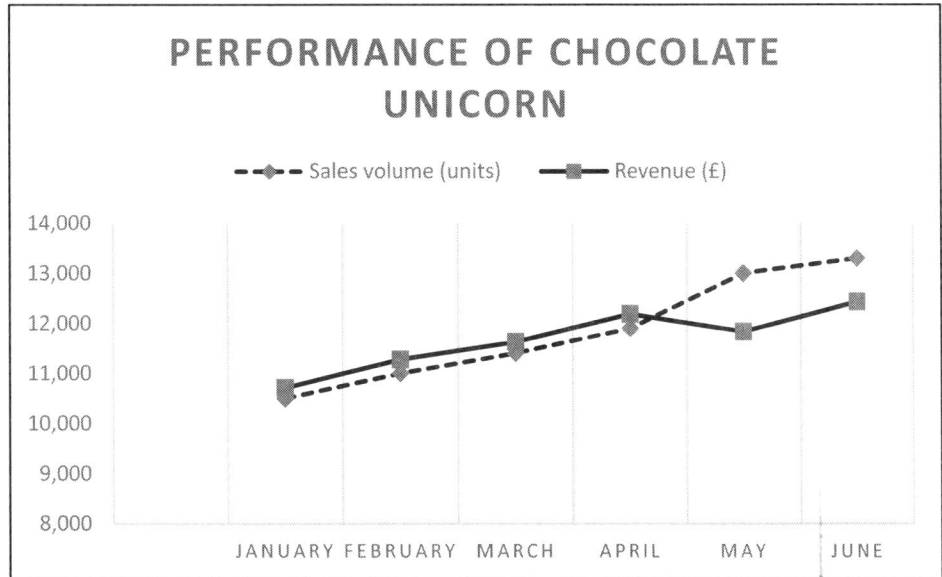

Explain the performance of the chocolate unicorn over the period concerned.

225 Hus Ltd is a tech company producing high-end "smart home" products in the UK. They manufacture and sell doorbells, cameras, and lights that can be connected to WiFi and controlled via the "Hus Home" smart phone app. Over the last few years, Hus Ltd has become the leading producer of smart doorbells in the UK.

Hus Ltd have been producing the doorbells and lights for a number of years, but only recently introduced the camera into their product range in 20X3.

All of the products are produced on separate production lines in different parts of the factory. Each production line has supervisors for each section of the production line. The lights production line currently has only one of the two supervisors needed, due to the retirement of an experienced supervisor in 20X3. Hus Ltd have struggled to recruit enough supervisors with the required experience, given they also needed to recruit supervisors for the new Camera production line at the same time. The remaining supervisor on the lights production line recently commented to senior management "I'm so stretched and overworked at the moment, I've been doing this job on my own for nearly 2 years now – when are we going to get someone else in?".

Hus Ltd operate in a highly competitive environment. The smart home industry in the UK includes major competitors Drench and Smarty, who both have similar products on the market. Drench appeals to the high-end market, and Smarty offers cheaper alternatives.

Senior management are using a dashboard reporting system to analyse the performance and operating data of the company, and they have asked you to comment on the following information provided in the dashboard:

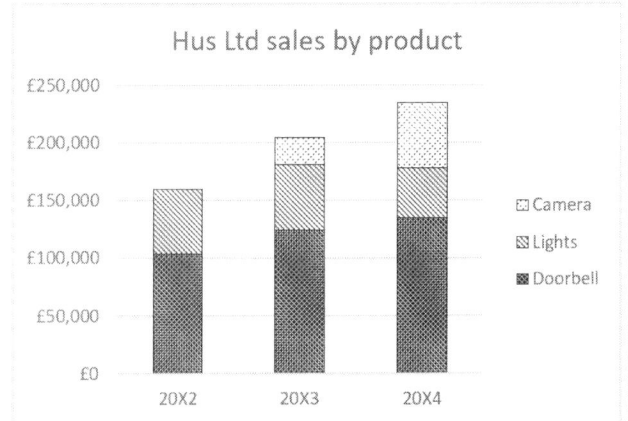

Operating Data for Hus Ltd (20X4):

Product	Doorbell	Lights	Camera
Supervisors on production line	3	1	2
Product returns	16	126	54
Customer complaints	2	86	12

Respond to senior management's requests by completing the following tasks:

(a) Using the data provided, identify on FOUR key findings relating to the performance of Hus Ltd, and explain a possible reason for each finding. Focus on both the performance of the company as a whole, and each product line.

(b) Identify TWO pieces of additional information that could improve your analysis.

Section 2

ANSWERS TO PRACTICE QUESTIONS

THE BUSINESS ORGANISATION

TYPES OF ORGANISATIONS

1 **Which of the following is NOT a key feature of an organisation?**

	✓
Controlled performance	
Collective goals	
Social arrangements	
Creation of a product	✓

Organisations do not have to create a product in order to be classified as an organisation. For example, an orchestra may be classed as an organisation, but it does not necessarily create a tangible product.

2 **Which ONE of the following organisations is normally found in the public sector?**

	✓
Schools	✓
Charities	
Clubs	
Businesses	

'Schools' is the correct answer because the other organisations are normally found in the private (i.e. non-governmental) sector.

AAT: BUSINESS AWARENESS

3 The public sector is normally concerned with which ONE of the following objectives?

	✓
Making profit from the sale of goods	
Providing services to specific groups funded from charitable donations	
The provision of basic government services	✓
Raising funds by subscriptions from members to provide common services	

The provision of basic government services is the main activity in the public sector. The first two options relate to the private sector and the last to a club.

4 Which ONE of these organisations would normally be classified as BOTH a not-for-profit organisation AND a private sector organisation?

	✓
Government departments	
Partnerships	
Charities	✓
Companies	

Partnerships and companies would both usually be profit seeking. While government departments are likely to be not-for-profit, they would be part of the public sector. Therefore only charities would be likely to be both private AND not-for-profit.

5 Which of the following best explains the reason for the improved performance of the combined entity?

	✓
Specialisation	
Social interactivity	
Synergy	✓
Service	

This is the definition of the term 'synergy'. Note that organisations may also allow specialisation, meaning that individuals can focus on becoming highly skilled in just one area.

ANSWERS TO PRACTICE QUESTIONS: SECTION 2

6 Identify whether each of the following statements is TRUE or FALSE.

Statement	True	False
Public limited companies are only owned by pension funds, trusts and other companies.		✓
A sole trader has unlimited personal liability for business debts.	✓	

Many plcs are listed on stock exchanges and hence shares can easily be bought by individuals as well as organisations.

With a sole trader, the owner 'is' the business, owns the assets and is liable for all the debts.

7 Identify whether each of the following statements is TRUE or FALSE.

Statement	True	False
Public limited companies have access to a wider pool of finance than partnerships or sole traders.	✓	
Both public and private limited companies are allowed to sell shares to the public.		✓

As public limited companies are able to sell their shares to the public, they will often find it easier to raise large amounts of capital for growth, if needed. This may be much harder for partnerships and sole traders.

Only public companies can sell shares to the public.

8 Identify whether each of the following statements is TRUE or FALSE.

Statement	True	False
Companies are always owned by many different investors.		✓
Shareholders are liable for any debts the company may incur.		✓

Companies may be owned by a single shareholder ('single member companies') or by many investors.

A company is a separate legal entity and thus liable for its own debts.

KAPLAN PUBLISHING

AAT: BUSINESS AWARENESS

9 Identify whether each of the following statements is TRUE or FALSE.

Statement	True	False
Not-for-profit organisations (NFPs) have varied objectives, which depend on the needs of their members or the sections of society they were created to benefit.	✓	
The primary objective of government-funded organisations is to reduce costs of their operations and thus minimise the burden on tax payers.		✓
Charities would usually be classified as a type of non-governmental organisation (NGO).	✓	

NFPs may have radically different objectives – a charity may aim to help, say, animals under threat of extinction while a hospital may wish to treat its patients as effectively as possible.

Government funded organisations are usually concerned with providing basic government services. This does not always involve minimising the costs of their operations.

NGOs are any organisations that do not have profit as a primary goal and are not directly linked to the government. Most charities would fall into this category.

10 Identify the correct type of organisation described in each of the following statements.

Statement	Sole trader	Public limited company	Unlimited liability partnership	Not-for-profit organisation
Owned by the shareholder(s)		✓		
The multiple owners have personal liability for business debts			✓	
Main objective is the provision of a service				✓
Can raise funds by issuing shares to the public		✓		

Note: for the second statement the key issues are (1) multiple owners, thus eliminating sole traders, and (2) personal liability. In these types of questions watch out for whether any partnerships listed have unlimited or limited liability.

ANSWERS TO PRACTICE QUESTIONS: SECTION 2

11 Identify the correct type of organisation described in each of the following statements.

Statement	Sole trader	Public limited company	Limited liability partnership	Not-for-profit organisation
May be financed via subscriptions by members				✓
The single owner has personal liability for business debts	✓			
Most likely to experience a separation between ownership and control		✓		

12 Identify whether each of the following statements concerning sole traders is TRUE or FALSE.

Statement	True	False
The owner must do all the work		✓
The owner has limited liability for unpaid business debts		✓
The business may borrow money using the sole trader's assets as security	✓	
The business has perpetual succession		✓

Many sole traders employ people to do some or all of the actual work in the business.

The proprietor is wholly liable for the debts of the business, borrowing money in their own name.

If a sole trader dies, the business's assets and liabilities form part of their estate but the business as such ceases to exist – there is no perpetual succession.

GOVERNANCE

13 Where there are a large number of external shareholders who play no role in the day-to-day running of a company, there is a situation that is described as:

	✓
Detached corporate ownership	
Uninvolved external ownership	
Dividend based shareholding	
Separation of ownership and control	✓

Reasons for the separation of ownership and control include the suggestion that specialist management can run the business better than those who own the business.

AAT: BUSINESS AWARENESS

14 The system of policies by which an organisation is directed and controlled is known as which ONE of the following?

	✓
Corporate governance	✓
Corporate social responsibility	
Corporate infrastructure	
Corporate strategic apex	

By definition.

15 Which ONE of the following is NOT a benefit of corporate governance?

	✓
Improved access to capital markets	
Stimulation of performance	
Enhanced marketability of goods and services	
Prevention of fraudulent claims by contractors	✓

Good governance will result in a better image with the providers of finance thus making raising finance easier.

Good governance should also result in sustainable wealth creation.

Customers will prefer to purchase a product or service from a company that has a strong reputation for good governance and hence lower levels of risk.

However, since corporate governance is the set of processes and policies by which the **company** is directed, administered and controlled, it will therefore not prevent fraudulent claims by an external party, i.e. contractors.

16 Which ONE of the following is NOT normally seen to be an objective of corporate governance?

	✓
Improving employee welfare	✓
Increasing disclosure to stakeholders	
Ensuring that the company is run in a legal and ethical manner	
Increasing the level of confidence in the company for investors and shareholders	

Although improving employee welfare is important, this is not seen as a primary objective of corporate governance.

ANSWERS TO PRACTICE QUESTIONS: SECTION 2

17 The 'agency problem' refers to which ONE of the following situations?

	✓
Shareholders acting in their own short-term interests rather than the long-term interests of the company	
A vocal minority of shareholders expecting the directors to act as their agents and pay substantial dividends	
Companies reliant upon substantial government contracts such that they are effectively agents of the government	
The directors acting in their own interests rather than the shareholders' interests	✓

Directors, who are placed in control of resources that they do not own and are effectively agents of the shareholders. They should be working in the best interests of the shareholders. However, they may be tempted to act in their own interests, for example by voting themselves huge salaries. The background to the agency problem is the separation of ownership and control – in many large companies the people who own the company (the shareholders) are not the same people as those who control the company (the board of directors).

TYPES OF FUNDING USED BY BUSINESSES

18 Identify the type of funding most likely to be described in each of the following situations.

	New capital introduced	Working capital	Loan	Retained profits
A project is financed by cutting a dividend				✓
A new partner is accepted into a partnership	✓			

19 Identify the type of funding most likely to be described in each of the following situations.

	New capital introduced	Working capital	Loan	Retained profits
A company delays paying suppliers		✓		
A finance package involves monthly interest payments			✓	

20 Identify whether each of the following statements made by the Chairman is TRUE or FALSE.

Statement by Chairman	True	False
"I don't think we should extend our overdraft facility as interest must be paid on the full facility"		✓
"The overdraft is repayable on demand making it a risky method of finance"	✓	

Interest is paid on the amount overdrawn, not the maximum possible overdraft allowed.

21 Which of the following is likely to be the most appropriate source of finance for Westeros?

	✓
Central government funding	
The existing owners of Westeros	✓
Issue of shares to the public	
Donations from the public	

Westeros is a profit-seeking organisation – given that its fifteen owners own 'shares', it must be a private limited company. As such, only B is likely to be appropriate from the options provided. Central government funding is usually for public sector organisations, donations would usually be the major source of funding for charities and Westeros cannot issues shares to the public as it is a private limited company.

22 For each of the following financing scenarios, identify whether the funding suggested would be appropriate.

Scenario	Funding	Appropriate?
A Ltd is looking to buy land and build a new factory.	Working capital	No
B Ltd is planning on investing in new plant and machinery to extend its production capacity to meet rising demand for its products.	Bank loan	Yes

A Ltd is looking at a long term investment, so some form of long term finance would be more appropriate.

B Ltd is buying new plant and machinery, which (1) is a longer term investment (2) could act as security, and (3) should result in steady cash inflows. Together this make a loan ideal.

ANSWERS TO PRACTICE QUESTIONS: SECTION 2

23 For each of the following financing scenarios, identify whether the funding suggested would be appropriate.

Scenario	Funding	Appropriate?
C Ltd has produced a cash flow forecast and has identified it will have a cash shortage for a two month period.	New share issue	No
D Ltd has reached its overdraft limit but still needs finance to buy a rival company.	Retained earnings	No

C Ltd is looking at a short term problem that needs financing, so some form of short term finance, such as via working capital, would be more appropriate.

D Ltd appears to have run out of cash, so will need external finance in order to buy a rival. Just having retained profits does not mean a company has cash as well.

24 For each of the following financing scenarios, identify whether the funding suggested would be appropriate.

Scenario	Funding	Appropriate?
ABC partnership wishes to buy a new building.	New share issue	No
X, a sole trader, needs to buy new fixtures and fittings.	New capital introduced	Yes

ABC is a partnership, so ownership is not represented through share ownership.

Provided they have sufficient funds, there is no reason why X cannot inject more funds into their business.

25 Identify whether each of the following statements is TRUE or FALSE.

	True	False
Interest payments on a loan can be suspended in the future if G is unable to afford them.		✓
Dividends are an allowable deduction against G's profits.		✓
G will likely need to provide asset security to investors whether it chooses to raise debt or equity finance.		✓

A company cannot normally suspend debt repayments if it can no longer afford them – this is only possible with dividends.

Dividends are not an allowable deduction, but interest is.

Finally, shareholders would not normally receive any security on their investment.

KAPLAN PUBLISHING

AAT: BUSINESS AWARENESS

26 Which ONE of the following sources of finance to companies is the most widely used in practice?

	✓
Bank borrowings	
Rights issues	
New share issues	
Retained earnings	✓

Retained earnings is the most widely used source of finance.

SERVICE BUSINESSES

27 Identify which quality of a service is described in each of the following statements.

Statement	Intangibility	Simultaneity	Heterogeneity	Perishability
The consumption of a service happens at the same time as the service delivery.		✓		
The quality of a service is harder to standardise, due to the person delivering the service.			✓	
A service does not, in itself, give the customer a physical product.	✓			
A service cannot be held in inventory to be used later when needed.				✓

28 Which of the following describes a characteristic of the services provided by an optician at VC Co during a standard appointment?

	✓
Tangible	
Homogeneous	
Non-perishable	
Simultaneous	✓

It is simultaneous (also known as 'inseparable'), as there is no delay between the service being provided by the optician and consumed by the patient.

The service would be described as intangible rather than tangible, variable rather than homogeneous, and perishable rather than non-perishable.

ANSWERS TO PRACTICE QUESTIONS: SECTION 2

29 Identify whether each of the following statements regarding United Training Ltd is TRUE or FALSE.

	True	False
It is more difficult to measure the quality of lecturers than it is to asses a physical product.	✓	
Effective staff recruitment and training are key ways of trying to ensure quality within United Training Ltd.	✓	
There is unlikely to be a link between staff utilisation and the perceived quality of courses.		✓

A physical product can be tested objectively against set criteria but the quality of a service will vary depending on the lecturer, their experience, whether their style suits the learners involved and so on. All these make evaluation more subjective.

Effective recruitment and training can ensure a degree of competence and standardisation.

There is likely to be a strong link between utilisation and quality. For example, a lecturer who has taught excessive numbers of courses may become more tired and, hence, less engaging in class.

THE LEGAL FRAMEWORK

REGULATION OF COMPANIES

30 Identify whether each of the following statements about the financial statements of limited companies is TRUE or FALSE.

	True	False
Financial statements should give a "true and fair" view of the position and performance of the company.	✓	
The term "true and fair" is precisely defined in UK company law.		✓

The CA2006 in the UK requires that financial statements are produced that give a true and fair view of the position and performance of the company.

The term 'true and fair' is not defined in company law.

31 Identify whether each of the following statements about the financial statements of limited companies is TRUE or FALSE.

	True	False
Companies are not required by law to maintain proper accounting records but do so because it is good practice.		✓
The detailed content and specification of "proper accounting records" is precisely defined in UK company law.		✓

Companies are required to maintain proper accounting records, which are sufficient to show and explain transactions.

The content of these records is not defined, but a record of transactions, assets and liabilities would be required as a minimum.

32 Identify whether each of the following statements about the financial statements of limited companies is TRUE or FALSE.

	True	False
Shareholders are responsible for the preparation of financial statements.		✓
Directors are responsible for the preparation of financial statements.	✓	
Auditors are responsible for the preparation of financial statements.		✓
Financial statements must be approved by the board of directors.	✓	

Directors are responsible for the preparation of financial statements and the board of directors must approve them.

33 Which ONE of the following parties has primary responsibility for ensuring that the financial statements of a limited company give a "true and fair" view?

	✓
Directors	✓
Chief accountant	
Auditors	
Everyone working in the finance department	

The Board of Directors is responsible for the financial statements giving a true and fair view. This responsibility cannot be delegated to others.

ANSWERS TO PRACTICE QUESTIONS: SECTION 2

34 Which ONE of the following characteristics of financial statements of a limited company is NOT normally required to ensure a "true and fair view"?

	✓
Does not contain any material misstatement	
Is 100% accurate	✓
Applies appropriate accounting standards	

The term 'true and fair' is not defined in company law, but normally means that the financial statements:

- follow all appropriate accounting standards
- contain information of sufficient quantity to satisfy the reasonable expectations of the users
- follow generally-accepted practice
- should not contain any material misstatement – the information should be reasonably accurate, and should not contain errors that would be large enough to alter the view of the company's affairs. However, this does not mean **100%** accurate.

35 Which of the following are consequences of separate legal entity?

(1) A company is fully liable for its own debts.

(2) A company owns its own property.

(3) A company enters into contracts in its own name.

	✓
(1) and (2) only	
(1) and (3) only	
(2) and (3) only	
(1), (2) and (3)	✓

36 Which of the following are characteristics of a COMPANY?

(1) A company has perpetual succession.

(2) A company is subject to the requirements of the Companies Act 2006.

(3) There is no separation of ownership and management in a company.

	✓
(1) and (2) only	✓
(1) and (3) only	
(2) and (3) only	
(1), (2) and (3)	

Companies often have a separation between ownership (shareholders) and control (companies are run by directors).

THE RIGHTS AND ROLES OF SHAREHOLDERS

37 Which ONE of the following is known as the system of that directs and controls the way in which a company is operated?

	✓
Companies Act 2006	
Corporate Governance	✓
Centralised Control	
Mission Statement	

38 Which ONE of the following is NOT a right of a shareholder?

	✓
To appoint a proxy	
To bring a derivative claim	
To vote on certain company affairs	
To recruit all members of staff	✓

Shareholders will delegate the day to day running of the company to directors, who will be responsible for the recruitment of staff.

THE ROLE AND DUTIES OF DIRECTORS

39 Which ONE of the following descriptions best describes what type of director Jess is?

	✓
An executive director	
A non-executive director	✓
A part-time director	
Not any type of director	

Non-executive directors are not involved in the day to day running of the company, they are part time, and provide an independent view.

40 Which ONE of the following is NOT a type of company director?

	✓
A supreme director	✓
A managing director	
An executive director	

ANSWERS TO PRACTICE QUESTIONS: **SECTION 2**

41 What is the minimum age of a director as required by Companies Act 2006?

	✓
16	✓
18	
21	

42 To whom does a director owe their statutory duties to?

	✓
The members	
The board of directors	
The company as a whole	✓

43 Which ONE of the following describes a director with day to day responsibility for running a company?

	✓
Chairman of the Board	
President	
Managing Director	✓

44 In the context of company law, what is Rebecca considered to be?

	✓
Managing director	✓
Operational Manager	
Non-executive director	
Chairman	

45 Identify whether each of the following statements about directors is TRUE or FALSE.

	True	False
The statutory duty of a director to disclose any interest that they have in a proposed transaction or arrangement with the company does not apply to non-executive directors.		✓
A director may not exercise their powers except for the purpose for which they were conferred.	✓	

Non-executive directors have the same statutory duties.

KAPLAN PUBLISHING

46 Which TWO of the following are statutory duties of a director?

	✓
To promote the success of the company	✓
To promote the relationship between directors and employees	
To declare trading losses to members	
To declare an interest in an existing transaction or arrangement	✓

47 In company law, which ONE of the following is NOT a statutory duty of directors?

	✓
Duty to act within their powers	
Duty to exercise independent judgement	
Duty to avoid conflicts of interest	
Duty to protect shareholder value	✓

48 Identify whether each of the following statements about directors is TRUE or FALSE.

	True	False
Directors' service contracts lasting more than one year must be approved by the members.		✓
Authority that flows for a person's position is known as "express" authority.		✓

Directors' service contracts lasting more than TWO years must be approved by the members. Authority that flows for a person's position is known as "implied" authority.

49 Identify whether each of the following statements about directors is TRUE or FALSE.

	True	False
Directors owe their duties to the company as a whole, not to individual members.	✓	
The director may be required to make good any loss suffered by the company.	✓	
Any property taken by the director from the company can be recovered from them if it is still in their possession.	✓	

ANSWERS TO PRACTICE QUESTIONS: SECTION 2

UNLIMITED LIABILITY PARTNERSHIPS

50 Identify whether each of the following statements concerning partnerships is TRUE or FALSE.

	True	False
There no formality required to create a partnership.	✓	
Partners in a partnership are personally liable for the debts of the firm.	✓	
Partnerships are not legally required to disclose their financial results to the general public.	✓	

51 Which ONE of the following is required to establish a general/ordinary partnership?

	✓
The partners obtain permission through Companies Act 2006	
The partners obtain permission from Companies House	
The partners simply agree to form the partnership	✓

52 Identify whether each of the following statements is TRUE or FALSE.

	True	False
The partners in an ordinary partnership jointly own the firm's assets.	✓	
The shareholders in a company jointly own the company's assets.		✓

A partnership is not a separate legal entity, whereas a company is.

53 What type of business does Karishma own?

	✓
Sole trader	✓
Limited company	
Partnership	

Where an individual is personally liable for the business debts, that person will be a sole trader.

54 Identify whether each of the following statements is TRUE or FALSE.

	True	False
The directors of a company are liable for any losses of the company.		✓
A sole trader business is owned by shareholders and operated by the proprietor.		✓
Partners are liable for losses in a partnership in proportion to their profit share ratio.	✓	
A company is run by directors on behalf of its members.	✓	

The directors of a company run the company; however, they are not personally liable for its losses. A sole trader business is owned and operated by the proprietor (sole trader).

Partners are jointly and severally liable for any losses of the business. The losses will be shared according to the profit share ratio in the partnership agreement.

A company is owned by the shareholders (members) and run by the directors/management team.

55 Identify whether each of the following statements is TRUE or FALSE.

	True	False
A partnership is a separate legal entity.		✓
A partnership is jointly owned and managed by the partners.	✓	
A partnership can raise capital by issuing shares to members of the public.		✓
A partnership is able to own property and other assets in its own name.		✓

A partnership is not a separate legal entity distinct from the partners and hence cannot own property in its own name.

ANSWERS TO PRACTICE QUESTIONS: SECTION 2

56 Identify whether each of the following statements is TRUE or FALSE.

	True	False
Both partnerships and limited liability companies are able to own assets in their own name.		✓
The members of a limited liability company have the right to participate in the management of that company, whereas partners do not have the right to participate in the management of their partnership.		✓
The partners have the right to participate in the management of the partnership, whereas members of a limited liability company do not have the right to participate in the management of that company.	✓	
Partnerships are subject to the same regulations regarding introduction and withdrawal of capital from the business as a limited liability company.		✓

A partnership is not a separate legal entity and hence cannot own property in its own name.

Shareholders do not have the right to participate in management.

Partnerships are subject to the Partnership Act 1890, whereas companies are subject to the Companies Act 2006.

57 Which of the following pairs of items would you expect to see in the financial statements of a partnership?

	✓
Dividends paid and Share premium account	
Capital accounts and Profit appropriation account	✓
Profit appropriation account and Dividends paid	
Share premium account and Capital accounts	

Dividends paid and share premium account apply only to limited company financial statements.

58 Which ONE of the following statements best summarises the legal position relating to the contract with Farms R Us?

	✓
J alone is liable because they acted without the other partners' authority.	
J, L and C are each personally liable, since partners are agents of each other.	
Top Farm & Co is liable as it was a contract entered into for the purposes of the partnership business.	
The firm and, therefore, all of its partners are liable on the contract to purchase 20 sheep from Farms R Us.	✓

Partners' acts in the usual course of business bind the firm and the partners.

KAPLAN PUBLISHING

STAKEHOLDERS

STAKEHOLDERS

59 Which THREE of the following would be considered to be connected stakeholders?

	✓
Employees	
Government	
Environmental pressure groups	
Suppliers	✓
Customers	✓
Lenders	✓

Connected stakeholders have a transaction with the business, such as suppliers, customers and lenders. Employees are internal stakeholders, whilst the government and environmental pressure groups are external stakeholders.

60 What are the three classifications of stakeholders commonly known as?

	✓
Internal, external, connected	✓
Shareholders, employees, customers	
Internal, external, regulated	
Connected, unconnected, external	

Internal stakeholders are those within the business, for example employees.

Connected stakeholders are those who have a transaction with the business, for example customers and suppliers.

External stakeholders are those outside of the business, for example the general public.

61 What approach is recommended for dealing with stakeholders in quadrant III of the above matrix?

	✓
Develop strategies that are fully acceptable to the stakeholder	
Keep the stakeholder satisfied	✓
Keep the stakeholder informed	
Minimum effort	

Stakeholders with low interest and high power can easily increase their level of interest which would make them key to any decisions being made. The best way to manage such stakeholders is to keep them satisfied in order to keep them from moving from quadrant III to quadrant IV.

ANSWERS TO PRACTICE QUESTIONS: SECTION 2

62 In respect of this move, which ONE stakeholder group from the following list would need to be kept informed?

	✓
Low-skilled employees (not heavily unionised)	✓
Customers (both UK and abroad)	
UK government (BetWalt's move is not against local laws)	
Major institutional investors (with shareholdings of between 25% and 30% each)	

Employees will be interested as the move affects their livelihoods, but have little power to stop the move.

Customers will have little interest as it will not affect their interaction with the company.

The UK government is likely to have little interest or power in the move of the company as it is not breaking any laws.

Major shareholders may be very interested as it impacts upon their investment. However, they would also have significant power and would thus be key players who expect to be involved in the decision, not just informed about it.

63 Employees are **internal** stakeholders, while finance providers are **connected** stakeholders.

Internal includes employees and managers/directors; connected includes shareholders, customers, suppliers, and finance providers. The third stakeholder group is external which includes the community at large, government and trade unions.

64 Using Mendelow's matrix, identify which ONE of the following responses would be appropriate for this stakeholder group.

	✓
Minimal effort	
Keep informed	
Keep satisfied	✓
Key players	

In this case, A's shareholders have a high level of power, but a low level of interest.

65 Identify whether the following statement is TRUE or FALSE.

Statement	True	False
A company is using a communication strategy aimed at explaining the rationale behind its actions to its stakeholders. Using Mendelow's matrix, these stakeholders would be categorised as 'minimal effort'.		✓

This approach is referred to as Keep Informed, whereas minimal effort implies that stakeholders will accept what they are told.

AAT: BUSINESS AWARENESS

66 Identify whether the following statement is TRUE or FALSE.

Statement	True	False
The interests of customers and shareholders can often appear to conflict – for example in the quality of goods and services.	✓	

This is correct as customers have an interest in higher levels of product and service quality and, in the short term at least, satisfying this interest is likely to reduce the profits and dividends available to shareholders.

67 For each of the four stakeholder groups listed below, identify whether they have high or low interest, and high or low power.

	Interest		Power	
	Low	High	Low	High
Customers		✓	✓	
Government		✓		✓
Shareholders		✓	✓	
Employees	✓		✓	

Customers will have high interest as price rises may force them out of business, but have little power as they have little alternative but to buy from FFD.

The Government of T has already taken a high interest in the situation and has vowed to do whatever is necessary to protect farmers.

Shareholders may be very interested having invested significant personal sums. However, they would have low individual power due to only having small individual shareholdings. Were they to work together, then collectively their power would become high.

Employees will be uninterested as the price rise will not directly affects their livelihoods, and have little power to influence the pricing decision.

68 Part (i): For each of the following, indicate whether they are internal, connected or external stakeholders.

Stakeholder	Internal	External	Connected
Kidsplay's management committee	✓		
The three building companies			✓
Local residents		✓	

Internal includes employees and managers; connected includes shareholders, customers, suppliers, and finance providers. The third stakeholder group is external which includes the community at large, government and trade unions.

Part (ii): For each of the stakeholder groups listed below, identify whether they have high or low interest, and high or low power.

	Interest		Power	
	Low	High	Low	High
The three building companies		✓	✓	
Local residents		✓		✓
The government charity regulator	✓			✓

The building companies will have high interest in the project going ahead and the possibility of winning a contract, but have little influence over the decision.

Local residents have already taken a high interest in the plan and oppose it. Having three politicians on the residents' committee gives them power to influence the decision.

The regulator is unlikely to take much interest in the plans, especially as they have a history of agreeing with the committee. However, should they wish to exercise it, they have significant power to impact charity decisions.

69 FCC is a large bank. Which TWO of the following would be classified as connected stakeholders for FCC?

	✓
FCC's shareholders	✓
FCC's employees	
Customers who borrow money from FCC	✓
FCC's managers and directors	
The government banking regulator	
The trade union representing FCC's employees	

Connected stakeholders either invest in or have dealings with FCC.

Employees and managers are internal stakeholders, while the regulator and trade union are external stakeholders.

70 Match the stakeholder with their need/expectation of the company.

Stakeholder	Need/expectation
Employees	Pay, working conditions and job security
Shareholders	Dividends and capital growth
Government	Provision of taxes and jobs and compliance with legislation
Customers	Value-for-money products and services

ORGANISATIONAL STRUCTURE

ORGANISATIONAL STRUCTURE AND GOVERNANCE

71 Which ONE of the following statements regarding the entrepreneurial structure is correct?

	✓
It usually allows for defined career paths for employees	
It often enjoys strong goal congruence throughout the organisation	✓
It can normally cope with significant diversification and growth	
Control within the organisation tends to be weak	

Because the entrepreneurial structure is run by one person who makes all the decisions, this powerful individual will have strong control over the organisation and its strategic direction, leading to better goal congruence.

72 Which ONE of the following is a disadvantage of a functional structure?

	✓
Lack of economies of scale	
Absence of standardisation	
Specialists feel isolated	
Empire building	✓

Function managers may make decisions to increase their own power, or in the interests of their own function, rather than in the interests of the company overall. Economies of scale, standardisation and specialists feeling comfortable are advantages of a functional structure.

73 Which ONE of the following structures is best placed to address the need for co-ordination between different functions in very complex situations?

	✓
Functional	
Divisional	
Matrix	✓
Geographical	

A matrix structure aims to combine the benefits of decentralisation (e.g. speedy decision making) with those of co-ordination. The more rigid structure in a divisional company would not have the necessary flexibility.

ANSWERS TO PRACTICE QUESTIONS: SECTION 2

74 Which ONE of the following structures results in a potential loss of control over key operating decisions and a reduction in goal congruence?

	✓
Matrix	
Entrepreneurial	
Functional	
Geographical	✓

The granting of authority over each geographic area to geographic bosses results in a potential loss of control over key operating decisions. This weakness is also present in a Divisional structure.

75 In relation to organisational structures which ONE of the following is the correct definition of the phrase 'span of control'?

	✓
The number of employees that a manager is directly responsible for	✓
The number of management levels in an organisational structure	
The number of levels in the hierarchy below a given manager	
The number of managers in the organisation	

The span of control is the number of people for whom a manager is directly responsible. Scalar chain relates to the number of management levels within an organisation.

76 Identify the correct type of structure described by each of the following characteristics.

Characteristic	Entrepreneurial	Functional	Divisional	Matrix
Structured in accordance with product lines or divisions or departments			✓	
Requires dual reporting to managers, for example when a project team member has to report to a project manager as well as a head of their functional department				✓
Built around the owner manager, who makes all the decisions	✓			
Appropriate for small companies which have few products and locations and which exist in a relatively stable environment		✓		

KAPLAN PUBLISHING

77 Which of the following organisational structures would be most appropriate for H Ltd to adopt?

	✓
Divisional	✓
Matrix	
Entrepreneurial	
Functional	

If H wants to manage each product separately, it will need to adopt either a matrix or divisional approach, as these would allow the creation of separate divisions for each product. However, H wishes to keep its administrative costs as low as possible. As the matrix structure has high admin costs due to high numbers of managers, A should adopt a divisional approach.

78 Which ONE of the following factors would tend to allow an organisation to develop a wide span of control?

	✓
Highly skilled, motivated employees	✓
Employees spread over a wide geographical area	
Employees undertake complex, changing tasks	

A wide span of control means that each manager looks after many staff members. This is easier if the staff members are skilled and motivated as they will require little supervision. However, if staff are widely spread or have to undertake complex tasks, it will be harder for a manger to look after them meaning that the span of control will tend to narrow.

79 Identify whether each of the following statements relating to organisational structure is TRUE or FALSE.

	True	False
A scalar chain refers to the number of levels of management within the organisation.	✓	
Entrepreneurial structures typically suffer from slow decision making.		✓
An organisation's span of control is unaffected by the nature of the work the organisation undertakes.		✓

Entrepreneurial structures tend to result in quicker decision making as the owner/manager may make most of those decisions.

The nature of the work can have a big impact on the span of control – for example, highly complex tasks will require more supervision by managers and smaller spans of control.

ANSWERS TO PRACTICE QUESTIONS: SECTION 2

80   Identify whether each of the following statements relating to organisational structure is TRUE or FALSE.

	True	False
Decentralisation tends to reduce training costs within the organisation.		✓
A matrix structure may increase conflict between managers.	✓	
Tall organisations typically have a narrow span of control.	✓	

Decentralisation can result in duplication and training economies may be lost.

81   Identify whether each of the following statements relating to a matrix structure is TRUE or FALSE.

	True	False
A matrix structure combines the benefits of decentralisation and co-ordination.	✓	
Within a matrix structure, employees will have dual reporting lines.	✓	
A matrix structure is largely theoretical and is rarely used in practice.		✓
A matrix structure should lead to less duplication across projects and therefore save money.	✓	

The matrix structure is commonly used in many industries, especially engineering, construction and consulting.

82   Which of these are advantages of the centralisation of decision-making within an organisation?

	✓
(i) and (ii) only	
(i), (ii) and (iii) only	
(iii) only	
(i) and (iv) only	✓

Centralisation involves most decisions being made centrally within the organisation (i.e. at head office level). This means less training for more junior/local staff as well as better goal congruence as all decisions within the organisation are made by the same, senior group of managers. Options (ii) and (iii) are advantages of **de**centralisation.

AAT: BUSINESS AWARENESS

83 Which ONE of the following characteristics of F plc would make decentralisation more difficult to implement?

	✓
It has many employees working in various locations	
It operates in many different market sectors	
All managers are very comfortable using modern technologies	
Some senior managers have an authoritative leadership style	✓

The senior managers with an authoritative leadership style are unlikely to want to let go of control, making decentralisation more difficult.

84 Which ONE of the following factors concerning G plc directly limits how many subordinates should report to a single manager?

	✓
The size of the business	
The length of the scalar chain	
Where in the organisational hierarchy the manager is placed	
The extent to which the manager has other responsibilities, such as dealing with customers and suppliers	✓

A manager with extensive other responsibilities, such as dealing with customers and suppliers, will have less time to manage staff, thus limiting their span of control.

THE ROLE OF THE FINANCE FUNCTION

85 Complete the following sentences by placing one of the following options in the spaces.

The preparation of forecasts, for example of future sales or material prices, will be an important role of the finance function in **enabling** the organisation to create and preserve value.

The preparation of comprehensive reports for shareholders will be an important role of the finance function in **narrating** how the organisation creates and preserves value.

The preparation of variance analysis for control purposes will be an important role of the finance function in **shaping** how the organisation creates and preserves value.

ANSWERS TO PRACTICE QUESTIONS: **SECTION 2**

86 Which role of the finance function best describes what Stan is doing?

	✓
Resource allocation	✓
Performance management and control	
Planning	
Financial (corporate) reporting	

Staffing numbers is part of resource allocation – an important role of the finance function will be working out which resources the organisation will require to achieve its objectives.

87 Which of the following statements is/are true?

	✓
Statement (i)	
Statement (ii)	
Both of them	
Neither of them	✓

Both these statements are false. The 'narrates how' role involves financial (corporate) reporting, the 'shapes how' role includes performance management and control.

The finance function should attempt to anticipate potential changes and be ready to respond.

88 Which ONE stakeholder of the finance function is most likely to require data on competitors' pricing strategies?

	✓
Sales	✓
Production	
Shareholders	
Employees	

The sales function would require live data on competitors' pricing and market trends to enable them to set selling prices.

89 Which ONE stakeholder of the finance function is most likely to require data on employee productivity?

	✓
Production	
Employees	
HR	✓
Shareholders	

The HR function requires data to incorporate appraisal systems, productivity analysis as well as collecting data on internal progressions and training days.

90 Which ONE stakeholder of the finance function is most likely to require data on market trends?

	✓
Employees	
Sales	✓
Production	
Shareholders	

Sales will, for example, require live data on competitors' pricing and market trends and will require metrics on key customer feedback about products and services.

91 Identify whether each of the following statements relating to the management accounting function is TRUE or FALSE.

	True	False
It is often used by external stakeholders, such as shareholders		✓
It is a requirement for all limited companies		✓
It is mainly a historic record of the organisation's activities		✓
It aids planning and decision making within the business	✓	

The other three are correct for financial accounting.

ANSWERS TO PRACTICE QUESTIONS: **SECTION 2**

92 Which ONE of the following KPIs is the best for measuring efficiency in the operations of the toy retailer?

	✓
Percentage on time delivery to customer	
The total level of sales compared to budget	
Percentage on time despatch of goods to customers	✓
Reorder rate from customers	

All the business can do is despatch on time once an order is made. Delivery itself is outside its control (first answer). Sales can go up for many reasons other than efficiency of operations – lower prices, for example (second answer). Equally, a customer may well order again and that could be a reflection of efficiency, but it could be a reflection of other factors such as cheap pricing for example (last answer).

93 Which ONE of the following is an example of co-ordination between the finance function and production?

	✓
Establishing credit terms	
Advising on prices	
Determining sales quantities	
Budgeting	✓

Production will decide how many items of what type are to be produced. The cost of producing these will be determined by the finance function and production together, and incorporated into the overall budget.

94 Which ONE of the following is a way in which an organisation's marketing department would co-ordinate with its finance function?

	✓
Calculating charge out rates for services provided by the organisation	✓
Calculating the budgets for the number of units to be produced	
Estimation of the costs of the raw materials required for production	
Decisions on the quality of raw materials that the organisation can afford to use	

The first option would most likely be a marketing or service provision crossover with the finance function. The other options relate to co-ordination between the production department and the finance function.

KAPLAN PUBLISHING

AAT: BUSINESS AWARENESS

95 In which ONE of the following ways would this department co-ordinate with E's finance function?

Decisions on the quantity of raw materials required	
Establishing credit terms for customers	
Calculating pay rises for staff	
Decisions on the selling price of the product	✓

The finance function can help ensure a profitable selling price is used for E's products.

96 Identify which TWO pieces of information G's finance department is likely to receive directly from the HR function rather than from the Operations function.

	✓
Expense claims for production mangers	
Time sheets for production workers	
Overtime rates for production workers	✓
A production supervisor's retirement date	✓

RISK

97 Which one of the following sentences best describes risk?

	✓
The exposure to the adverse consequences of dangerous environments.	
The expected impact of uncertain future events on objectives.	✓
The chance of being caught doing something unethical.	
The impact of the exposure to the adverse consequences of uncertain future events.	

A full definition of risk should allow for both upside and downside aspects and incorporate the concepts of both probability and impact.

ANSWERS TO PRACTICE QUESTIONS: SECTION 2

98 Risk management is the process of reducing the adverse consequences either by reducing the _____ of an event or its _____.

What are the two missing words?

	✓
Understanding and impact	
Likelihood and potential	
Understanding and potential	
Likelihood and impact	✓

Risk management is the process of reducing the adverse consequences either by reducing the likelihood of an event or its impact.

99 Match each of the following risks to the appropriate risk category.

Risk category	Risk
Business risks	Raw material prices rise
Economic risks	Disposable income levels fall
Corporate reputation risks	CEO convicted of illegal share dealing
Political risks	Increased regulation of an industry

100 Match each of the following risks to the appropriate risk category.

Risk category	Risk
Political risks	Change of Government
Legal risks	Customer sues company for negligence
Regulatory risks	Government increases rate of Corporation Tax
Compliance risks	Company prosecuted for breach of the Data Protection Act

101 The sudden death of the CEO of a small marketing consultancy would best fit which category in a risk map?

	✓
Low probability; low impact	
Low probability; high impact	✓
High probability; low impact	
High probability; high impact	

Particularly because it is a small consultancy firm, the death of the CEO would be high impact. However, unless there is a known condition, the probability of sudden death is low.

KAPLAN PUBLISHING

102 The resignation of a member of the sales staff would best fit which category in a risk map?

	✓
Low probability; low impact	
Low probability; high impact	
High probability; low impact	✓
High probability; high impact	

High staff turnover is common in the industry so probability is high.

Losing one sales person in a large organisation is unlikely to be anything other than low impact.

103 The 'TARA' mnemonic is often used to categorise risk management methods. Which one of the following represents the methods in the TARA mnemonic?

	✓
Transfer; Assure; Remove; Accept	
Transfer; Accept; Reduce; Adapt	
Transfer; Avoid; Reduce; Accept	✓
Transfer; Accept; Remove; Adapt	

104 Which ONE of the following strategies is Metherell Ltd using to manage its risk exposure?

	✓
Risk avoidance	
Risk reduction	
Risk transfer	✓
Risk acceptance	

The insurance policy transfers the risk to the insurance company.

Avoidance would imply not launching the product.

Reduction would imply taking action to prevent any chance of a leak.

Acceptance would imply doing nothing and just proceeding to launch the product.

ANSWERS TO PRACTICE QUESTIONS: SECTION 2

105 Identify which strategy best describes the following risk management approaches.

	Transfer	Accept	Reduce	Avoid
A race event BAS has organised for next week is an outdoors 5k run. However if it rains it is unlikely to attract enough competitors to make any profit. The management have decided to still hold the event.		✓		
BAS has just taken out a large insurance contract to ensure they are covered if any competitor seeks damages for injuries caused in one of their races.	✓			
One of the employees at BAS has had an innovative idea to hold a waterfall jumping event where competitors compete to jump from the highest possible place along a sheer cliff edge into the North Sea. After considering the idea the BAS management have rejected it as it is too dangerous.				✓
As part of the organisation of the huge annual showcase event BAS holds, the managers have conducted a large and extensive risk assessment process and put into place all the internal controls they believe to be necessary.			✓	

106 Identify which TWO of the following responses to this risk would be most appropriate.

	✓
Keep monitoring the situation	
Accept the risk and continue to operate as normal	
Make sure that good insurance is in place	✓
Outsource the IT function	✓
Close departments that would be the most affected by an IT breakdown	

Monitoring the situation and/or accepting the risk would be suitable responses if the risk was regarded as having low potential impact and low probability. Here we have high impact.

For a risk that is of high potential impact but low probability, sharing the risk by making sure that there is insurance cover is important. Similarly, outsourcing the IT function might help in reducing the risk, as long as there is a service level agreement (SLA) in place which protects the hospital in the event of system breakdowns.

Closing the affected departments is an example of avoidance of the risk, which would be more appropriate if the risk was viewed as having high impact and high probability.

AAT: BUSINESS AWARENESS

107 Assess the significance of the risk to OKJ of each of the factors described below.

Factor	Significance
OKJ's home country has recently elected a new government. It is not yet clear if they will introduce new legislation to increase minimum wages. This would have a major impact on OKJ's profitability.	The new government falls into the category of high-impact, high-uncertainty – it is uncertain whether the government will put in place minimum wage legislation but this could have a significant impact on the company's profits. OKJ definitely needs a contingency plan for this.
After a recent accident in one of its factories, OKJ was convicted of breaching relevant health and safety legislation. Based on similar recent cases brought in the industry, OKJ expects to be fined around 7% of its turnover. OKJ has insurance in place that will cover this fine.	The accident is relatively low impact (thanks to OKJ's insurance) and low uncertainty (OKJ seems confident that it will have to pay the fine), so no further action is needed to manage the risk.
OKJ uses platinum as a key component within some of its products. The price of metals varies significantly on world markets and tends to rise sharply in times of recession. The directors are concerned that its products may become unprofitable if platinum prices rise more than 20% from their current levels, but is uncertain about whether this would happen – even if a recession does occur.	Platinum price rises are high impact (the cost of platinum rising sharply could cause a fall in profits) and high uncertainty (the movement in metal prices is uncertain, as is the likelihood of a recession). OKJ may wish to consider contingency plans here – such as entering into fixed price contracts if possible.
OKJ is uncertain about whether it can retain its CEO in the long term. It has had a number of CEO's over the last five years – each of them staying very different lengths of time in their roles. Fortunately, OKJ has an experienced Board of Directors and the change in CEOs has had little impact on the business in the past.	The status of the CEO appears to be highly uncertain (it is not clear how long the CEO will stay with the company), but low impact (the remaining Board of Directors is capable of minimising disruption to the company), so again this is unlikely to be considered a high risk factor.

108 Which ONE of the following statements concerning the difference between risk and uncertainty is true?

	✓
The term 'risk' is used when a business only considers potential adverse effects, whereas 'uncertainty' includes looking at potential gains.	
The term 'risk' is used when all possible outcomes can be quantified, whereas 'uncertainty' means future outcomes are unknown.	
The term 'risk' is used when probabilities can be estimated for possible outcomes, whereas 'uncertainty' means we cannot estimate probabilities.	✓
The term 'risk' is used when probabilities are certain, whereas 'uncertainty' means probabilities are only estimates.	

By definition.

ANSWERS TO PRACTICE QUESTIONS: **SECTION 2**

109 Explain TWO potential risks that could arise as a result of the new targets.

Possible risks could include the following (only two needed):

1	Surgeons will see the targets as unachievable and thus become demotivated by them.
2	Surgeons will rush operations, leading to poorer outcomes for patients and damage to the hospital's reputation.
3	Surgeons will demand that they will only work towards the new targets if they receive bonuses, increasing costs.
4	Surgeons will ignore the targets and do as they have always done and the new scheme will fail.

110 Evaluate the following risks to Q arising from the changes to health and safety laws:

Risk	Evaluation
Q's contractor costs may increase.	Q may need to source contractors from outside the local area, which is likely to increase costs.
Q may no longer be able to use recommended contractors.	Unless Q pays for the insurance, which seems unlikely, this will be the case.
There may be a shortage of contractors for Q to use leading to a backlog of work building up.	Since local contractors are unlikely to have the accreditation, there will be a shortage and work will back up.
Q may be unable to obtain the relevant insurance.	There does not appear to be a problem with Q getting the insurance but paying for it seems difficult.

EXTERNAL ANALYSIS

PESTLE

111 Which THREE of the following factors would be included in this analysis?

	✓
New sources of supply for tobacco	
Government commitments to reduce smoking among young people	✓
A merger of two rival companies	
A ban on smoking in public places	✓
An increase in tax on cigarettes	✓

The three factors highlighted would be classed as either political or legal factors within a PESTEL.

The first factor relates to supply within the market and the third to the degree of competition, so neither relates to the wider macro-environmental factors that a PESTLE would address.

112 Which ONE of the following factors would most likely be identified under the 'social' heading of a PESTLE analysis?

	✓
New CAD and CAM has recently become available for use in F's factories	
Recycling is increasingly important to the residents of country F	✓
Increased disposable income of consumers within country F	
Changes in minimum wage legislation within country F	

CAD/CAM would be a technological factor.

Disposable income would be an economic factor.

Minimum wage legislation could be viewed as either a legal or political factor.

113 Which ONE of the following would a transport company monitor under the 'political' heading as part of a PESTLE analysis?

	✓
Tracking systems to monitor driver hours/anti-theft devices/developments in tyre technology.	
State of the economy/oil price movements/a rise in interest rates.	
Fuel tax/congestion charges in cities/plans to build new roads.	✓
Predicted car numbers and usage/public concerns over safety.	

Tracking system = Technological heading,

State of economy = Economic heading,

Predicted car numbers = Social heading.

114 Which of these statements is/are correct?

	✓
(1) only	
(2) only	✓
Both	
Neither	

An aging population will not automatically mean that high-tech products will fall in popularity – though the businesses that manufacture and sell them may need to adjust their products and marketing to target older users.

The second statement is correct.

ANSWERS TO PRACTICE QUESTIONS: **SECTION 2**

115 What change in people's attitudes has put additional pressure on businesses to become more socially responsible?

	✓
Disposable income is growing as people have fewer children.	
More people are living in cities, encouraging companies to build more compact offices.	
Fashion changes rapidly therefore frequently change of suppliers becomes a necessity.	
People are more aware of the 'carbon footprint' left by a company's operations.	✓

Carbon footprint refers to the volume of carbon emissions produced by the company. The goal of social responsibility is to be conscious of the impact operations have on the environment and the planet. It is possible for the firm's products to be boycotted if customers believe that it acts in a socially irresponsible way.

116 Which TWO of the following are potential consequences for Q of a rise in interest rates?

	✓
Those customers who have purchased houses via government schemes may default on their loans.	
Q may find demand for its new houses decreases.	✓
Q's own costs may increase.	✓
The government may withdraw their schemes leading to a drop in demand.	
The cost of land will increase.	

The population of Q may be reluctant to purchase houses in a climate of interest rate rises despite government schemes. If Q has taken out loans to fund expansion (for example to purchase new machinery) costs will increase.

Customer defaults are a risk to the government, not to Q. The government are unlikely to withdraw schemes since their policy of encouraging people onto the housing ladder will not change. The cost of land will not necessarily increase if interest rates go up.

117 Identify THREE PESTLE categories and, for each category identified, explain how this may have an impact on the future performance of Bee Carpets Ltd.

PESTLE category	Impact
Political	National government policy affects the whole economy through changes to interest rates and/or taxation, and hence potential demand. Local government decisions could impact the choice of sales outlets, e.g. planning and site development – town centre or out-of-town developments.
Economic	The state of the UK economy will have a big impact on demand as carpets are a significant item of expenditure for most consumers. For example, a downturn in disposable incomes or a rise in interest rates would reduce demand for carpets overall, although this may mean people will want more of the cheaper range.
Social	An ageing population could mean ongoing, or even growing, demand for traditional products for many years. On the other hand longer term growth will depend on appealing to younger customers as well. Increased use of out of town retail parks and/or online shopping could increase the need for Bee Carpets to use channels other than high street retailers.
Technological	The use of technologies such as process automation and robotics could enable the new range to be manufactured with much lower labour costs, thus allowing lower prices to be set. The use of a website for sales could enhance the number of customers reached. However, the company will need to ensure it has strong cyber security measures in place.
Environmental	The use of oil-derived products is not sustainable and could undermine the Bee Carpets brand. Furthermore, the environmental impact of disposing of carpets at the end of their lives should also be considered as man-made fires are unlikely to be as easy to recycle as natural fabrics. It would be advisable to consider using cheaper natural fibres instead.
Legal	As well as the potential impact of changes in laws relating to manufacturing (e.g. Health and Safety legislation) and labour (e.g. a national minimum wage), the Directors would also need to ensure they comply with data protection laws, such as GDPR, for customers buying via the website.

Note: only THREE factors required.

ANSWERS TO PRACTICE QUESTIONS: SECTION 2

118 For each of the specified PESTLE categories given in the table below, explain how there may be a THREAT to the future performance of CCC Car Rentals, and explain ONE action the company could take to reduce each threat.

PESTLE category	Nature of threat		Action to reduce threat
Economic	1	The ongoing global recession may result in lower incomes and hence customers switching into the lower price, value segment. This will result in lost customers and reduced profitability.	CCC Car Rentals could diversify and start to offer cheaper low cost rentals within the value segment.
	2	The ongoing recession may result in increased competitive rivalry between car rental companies, such as involving price wars, thus reducing profitability.	CCC Car Rentals could try to reduce its cost base by closing less profitable rental outlets.
Technological	1	The company is reliant on gaining sales via its website and app. A cyber-attack, such as hacking or denial-of-service, could lose sales and damage the firm's reputation.	CCC Car Rentals should ensure it has good cyber-security on its website and app, ensuring that customer information is secure. As part of this it could consider outsourcing testing of its cyber-security processes.
	2	Customers for whom time is especially important, such as business users, may switch to rivals who have embraced new technologies, such as self-service kiosks.	CCC Car Rentals should monitor technological developments and invest in proven technologies as soon as possible, to ensure they remain as market leaders.

119 For each of the specified PESTLE categories given in the table below, explain ONE possible THREAT to the future performance of ZZZ Beds, and explain ONE action the company could take to reduce each threat.

PESTLE category	Nature of threat	Response
Technological	If rivals adopt greater automation, then this might reduce their cost of production, allowing them scope to reduce their prices compared to ZZZ Beds. This may make the company uncompetitive.	ZZZ Beds should assess whether automation affects quality. If quality is reduced through automation, then ZZZ Beds may choose to ignore/accept the threat. However, if quality is maintained, then ZZZ Beds should seek to adopt automation where possible.
Environmental	Customers are becoming increasingly concerned about green issues, so may switch to rivals with better environmental credentials, such as using recycled materials.	ZZZ Beds should audit its supply chain and choice of raw materials to assess their sustainability and change suppliers/materials if necessary. Furthermore it could introduce a recycling scheme for old mattresses.

120 For each of the specified PESTLE categories given in the table below, explain ONE possible THREAT to the future performance of Chokolate Box, and explain ONE response the company could take to each threat.

PESTLE category	Nature of threat	Response
Political	Given concerns over health issues surrounding chocolate, the UK Government may consider extending its 'sugar tax' to confectionary. This would damage Chokolate Box's reputation and increase prices to customers.	Chokolate Box will need to reduce the sugar content of its products and/or consider diversification into healthier products to reduce its risk exposure.
Economic	An increase in the value of the pound would make exported chocolates more expensive to foreign customers, thus reducing demand.	To some extent this risk is mitigated by a stronger pound also making imported raw materials, such as cocoa, cheaper. If prices are set in foreign currencies, such as US dollars, Chokolate Box could decide to limit price rises to foreign customers and accept reduced margins.

ANSWERS TO PRACTICE QUESTIONS: SECTION 2

THE MICRO-ECONOMIC ENVIRONMENT

121 Which ONE of the following best describes the concept of 'complementary goods'?

	✓
The purchase of one good means that a similar good is not purchased	
A number of goods exist, any of which can be purchased to satisfy a need	
One good is free and the other has to be paid for	
The purchase of one good leads to the purchase of another good	✓

By definition.

122 Which ONE of the following will cause the demand curve for a good to shift to the right?

	✓
The price of the good falls	
Disposable income increases	✓
The supply of the good increases	
The price of a substitute falls	

An increase in income normally results in an increase in demand.

Viewed in isolation, a fall in the price of a good will involve a movement along a demand curve but will not move the curve itself.

A change in supply will move the supply curve, not the demand curve.

If the price of a substitute falls, then demand for the substitute will increase and demand for the original good fall, as shown by the demand curve shifting to the left.

123 Which ONE of the following will cause the demand curve for a good to shift to the right?

	✓
A reduction in indirect tax on the good	
An improvement in production which lowers costs	
An increase in the price of the good	
An increase in the supply of a complementary good	✓

The first two refer to the supply curve.

A change in price causes a movement along the demand curve but does not shift the curve.

An increase in the supply of, and therefore the demand for, the complementary good would create an increase in demand for this product at all price levels (a shift to the right).

KAPLAN PUBLISHING

124 Which ONE of the following will NOT cause the supply curve for a good to shift to the right?

	✓
The receipt of a government subsidy	
An increase in employment costs	✓
Improvements in manufacturing technology	
Lower prices for raw materials	

A government subsidy, improvements in technology and lower material prices would all shift the supply curve to the right, as the company would be willing to make more items at a given price.

However, an increase in employment costs would shift the supply curve to the left.

125 Which ONE of the following would explain a rise in the price of a good accompanied by a fall in the quantity sold?

	✓
The supply curve shifting to the left	✓
The demand curve shifting to the right	
The demand curve shifting to the left	
The supply curve shifting to the right	

If the supply curve moves to the left while the demand curve is unchanged, then the new equilibrium will be at a point where the price is higher but the quantity lower.

This shown in the diagram below.

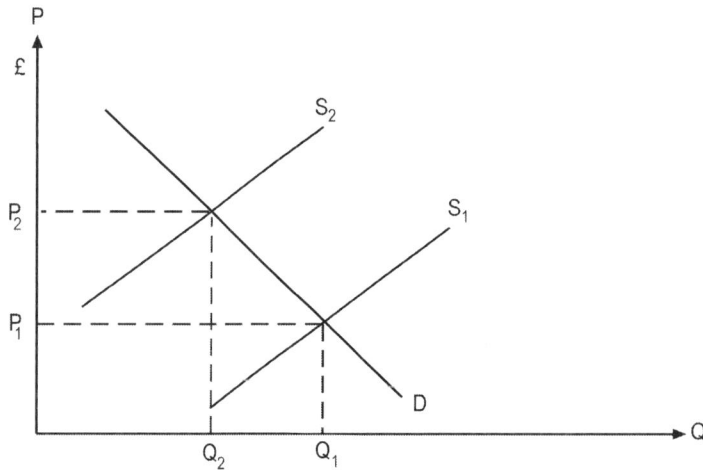

126 **The shift to the right in the supply curve can best be explained by which ONE of the following?**

	✓
An increase in the price of the product	
An increase in the price of raw materials	
A rise in the amount of wages paid to labour	
The result of technological progress	✓

Technological progress increases the efficiency of production and lowers costs, so producers will be willing to supply more items at a given price.

127 **What action will suppliers take at the price of P_{high}?**

	✓
Increase supply to take advantage of the high price	
Supply the same quantity of goods but at a reduced price	
Supply a reduced quantity of goods but at the same price	
Decrease price to attract more demand	✓

There is currently excess supply in the market; customers must be encouraged to purchase more of the good. The supplier needs to attract more demand – this can be done by decreasing price.

128 **Which ONE of the following best describes the concept of 'substitute goods'?**

	✓
The purchase of one good means that a similar good is not purchased	✓
A competitor providing the same good	
One good is free and the other has to be paid for	
The purchase of one good leads to the purchase of another good	

Substitute goods are similar goods (though not the same good) that consumers may purchase instead of our good.

129 **Which of the following is NOT held constant when we draw a demand curve?**

	✓
The price of complementary goods	
The price of substitutes	
Consumers' income	
The price of the good	✓

The price of the good itself is not held constant when we draw the demand curve.

130 A demand curve is drawn assuming all but one of the following remains unchanged. Which ONE item can vary?

	✓
Consumer tastes	
The price of the product	✓
The price of other products	
Disposable income	

A demand curve measures the quantity of a product that consumers will purchase at different price levels. Only the price of the product is allowed to vary to construct a demand curve.

131 Which ONE of the following statements best describes the movement from P_0 to P_1 in the diagram below?

	✓
An outward shift in the demand curve	
A fall in the supply of the good	
An expansion along the demand curve	✓
A fall in demand	

The line is downward sloping so must represent a demand curve. No supply curve is shown and so supply is unaffected. Moving from P_0 to P_1 represents a fall in price and a corresponding increase in demand. This is called an expansion along the demand curve as the demand curve has not shifted.

132 What will the new equilibrium price be if there is an increase in the price of cocoa beans?

	✓
V	
W	✓
X	
Y	
Z	

The cost of supply will increase, moving the supply curve upwards and to the left; demand is unchanged.

ANSWERS TO PRACTICE QUESTIONS: SECTION 2

SUSTAINABILITY

133 Which of the following would best explain the concept of sustainable development?

	✓
Starting business in the developed countries where the economic climate is conducive to trade.	
Development which meets the needs of the present without compromising the ability of future generations to meet their own needs.	✓
Sustaining the production at the level of maximum capacity.	
Developing the business by signing long-term contracts with suppliers.	

Sustainable development focuses on meeting the needs of the present without compromising the ability of future generations to meet their own needs.

134 Which TWO of the following are possible problems caused by a CSR policy??

	✓
Increased materials cost	✓
Failure to attract and retain quality employees	
Loss of management time	✓
Loss of key business skills	

CSR is likely to attract good quality employees and should not lead to a loss of key skills within the organisation. However, goods need to be purchased from ethical sources, which may lead to a rise in their cost. It can also take up significant amounts of management time, which could have been used to increase business profits.

135 A Ltd is considering improving its impact on the environment by adopting a sustainable approach to business.

Identify whether each of the following statements relating to A's decision is TRUE or FALSE.

	True	False
It may help to reduce the organisation's operating costs	✓	
It could lead to an improved relationship with shareholders and other stakeholders	✓	
It may improve employee motivation	✓	
It would be expected to reduce the administrative burden on management		✓

Ensuring sustainability may require a significant amount of management time and attention, which is unlikely to reduce their administrative burden.

136 Which ONE of the following would be most helpful to Choke in minimising the impact that wastage of material G has on the environment?

	✓
Sourcing raw materials from environmentally friendly suppliers	
Improved communication with customers to identify likely demand	✓
Improved energy efficiency of the production process for material G	
Reduction in packaging on the units of material G that are sold	

While all four options would improve the overall environmental impact of the company, only the second would actually reduce the amount of wastage of G itself. By trying to predict demand accurately, the company can make only as much G as is needed, thereby reducing wastage.

137 Identify the correct type of sustainability that each of the following policies relates to.

Policy	Social sustainability	Environmental sustainability	Financial sustainability
A Ltd aims to be carbon neutral across all of its operations within 3 years.		✓	
B Ltd has detailed financial and non-financial targets to ensure it can achieve its strategic plans to grow shareholder wealth.			✓
C Ltd offers all employees opportunities for advancement, training and CPD.	✓		

138 Which of the following is NOT a way in which businesses can reduce the amount of damage they cause to the environment?

	✓
Rebranding of products	✓
Recycling	
Redesigning products to use fewer materials	
Careful production planning	

Merely rebranding a product is unlikely to reduce a company's impact on its environment. The other three, however, should all help.

ANSWERS TO PRACTICE QUESTIONS: SECTION 2

139 Is this statement TRUE or FALSE?

	✓
True	✓
False	

By not creating waste, an organisation is ensuring that resources are more likely to be available to future generations, improving sustainability.

140 Which of the following statements best describes' corporate social responsibility'?

	✓
A company should play an active part in the social life of the local neighbourhood.	
A company should be sensitive to the needs of all stakeholders.	✓
A company should be alert to the social needs of all employees.	
A company should act responsibly in relation to shareholders' overall needs – not just their financial needs.	

The stakeholders are all those influenced by, or those who can influence the company's decisions and actions.

141 Identify whether each of the following statements relating to sustainability is TRUE or FALSE.

	True	False
Sustainability involves taking a long-term view and allowing the needs of present generations to be met without compromising the ability of future generations to meet their own needs.	✓	
Sustainability involves considering the needs of the organisation's shareholders only.		✓
Accountants have a public interest duty to protect society as a whole and the organisation's sustainability.	✓	

Sustainability involves considering the needs of the organisation's wider stakeholders, not just its shareholders.

AAT: BUSINESS AWARENESS

142 Which ONE of the following statements best describes the actions MLC should take in the light of this?

	✓
Place more orders with the supplier – it's cheap labour so the margins are good, which should keep the shareholders happy.	
Leave things as they are and hope the information doesn't get out.	
Continue trading with the supplier but investigate the claims quietly.	
Cancel all contracts with the supplier and release a press statement stating how the company will always act quickly and decisively if unethical practices are suspected.	✓

MLC have clearly marketed themselves as an ethical company and will therefore attract shareholders who are looking for ethical investments and customers looking for ethically produced goods. If they continue trading with this supplier then their reputation will suffer if the news gets out. By taking strong decisive action and controlling the news story they have demonstrated that they follow their stated ethical principles.

143 Which THREE of the following are common arguments FOR organisations adopting a strong commitment to sustainability?

	✓
Increased profitability due to cost reductions	
Faster strategic decision-making	
Improved reputation with environmentally conscious customers	✓
Ability to attract higher calibre staff	✓
Reduced risk of government intervention in the future	✓

A strong commitment to sustainability may save on some costs, such as energy costs due to lower energy usage. However, other costs may increase, such as purchasing costs as the organisation has to source its goods more carefully.

There is no reason why a commitment to sustainability would speed up decision making in the organisation – in fact it is likely to use up management time that could be spent helping to earn the business higher profits.

However, a commitment to sustainability often helps to attract both customers and staff, and reduces that chance that governments will be forced to regulate against unethical business behaviour in future.

144 FOR EACH of the Triple Bottom Line reporting headings suggest TWO ways that a mining company such as Tio Rino can be a sustainable mining company.

People

- Provide a safe and healthy workplace for employees where their rights and dignity are respected.

- Build enduring relationships with local communities and neighbours that demonstrate mutual respect, active partnership, and long-term commitment.

- Improve safety record re accident, fatalities.

- Develop health programmes for local communities – e.g. in respect of AIDS/HIV in some African countries.

- Ensure that if communities need to be moved or relocated, that resettlement and compensation are generous and cultural heritage is not compromised.

- Invest in people over the long term by fostering diversity, providing challenging and exciting work and development opportunities, and rewarding for performance.

- Ensure post-mining land use is discussed with local communities and is consistent with their aims and needs.

Profit

- Pay taxes without finding loopholes to avoid them.

- Ensure local communities benefit in terms of employments and a share of overall profits.

- Reinvest in local communities and projects rather than taking all profits back to the mining company's home country.

Planet

- Wherever possible prevent – or otherwise minimise, mitigate and remediate – harmful effects of activities on the environment.

- Avoid developing sites where the risk to biodiversity is particularly high.

- Develop new ways to reduce emissions of dangerous gases such as SO2 and NO2.

- Plant new trees elsewhere to replace ones felled for mining to ensure biodiversity.

- Landscape and replant sites after mining has finished. Pay for species to be repopulated.

- Use offsetting schemes to compensate for emission of greenhouse gases (e.g. schemes to plant additional trees somewhere else).

- Develop ways to process waste to avoid polluting the surrounding water system.

- Reducing energy usage by more efficient processes.

- Recycle as much waste products as possible.

Note: only TWO needed for each heading.

ETHICS

ETHICS

145 Indicate which fundamental ethical principle is under threat. Select ONE answer only.

	✓
Integrity	
Confidentiality	
Professional competence and due care	✓
Professional behaviour	
Objectivity	

146 (i) Indicate which fundamental ethical principle is under threat. Select ONE answer only.

	✓
Integrity	
Confidentiality	
Professional competence and due care	
Professional behaviour	✓
Objectivity	

(ii) Indicate what course of action Bella should take.

	✓
Do nothing – a sign is not worth losing your job over	
Suggest to the FD that they should replace the sign	✓

147 (i) Indicate which fundamental ethical principle is under threat. Select ONE answer only.

	✓
Integrity	
Confidentiality	✓
Professional competence and due care	
Professional behaviour	
Objectivity	

ANSWERS TO PRACTICE QUESTIONS: SECTION 2

(ii) Indicate your best course of action.

	✓
From an ethical point of view you should tell your friend about the redundancies on the grounds it could save them unnecessary financial problems and distress.	
You should not tell your friend about the redundancies.	✓

You should not tell your friend about the redundancies as to do so would breach confidentiality.

148 Which ONE of the following is NOT an appropriate course of action to take next?

	✓
Contacting AAT's ethical helpline for advice	
Reporting the company to the environment agency	
Contacting a journalist at a national newspaper	✓
Taking the matter to the Audit committee	

The basic principle here is that of confidentiality. To go outside of the business and professional environment in this manner without first considering the other options presented would not be following recommended process.

AAT's ethics helpline exists to give members advice and is not a breach of confidentiality as it is within the professional arena.

Reporting the company to the environment agency would comply with relevant legislation, however you would need to sure of your facts before whistle blowing.

The Audit committee should be all NEDs and therefore a logical place to go, particularly as they are also responsible for the whistle blowing policy.

149 'The principle of confidentiality imposes an obligation on Alessandro to refrain from which ONE of the following?

	✓
using the information to the advantage of Sueka LLP'	✓
disclosing the information within Sueka LLP'	
disclosing the information to anyone at Polina Ltd'	

The principle of confidentiality imposes an obligation on Alessandro to refrain from using the information to the advantage of Sueka LLP.

150 Indicate which TWO fundamental ethical principles are under threat.

	✓
Integrity	
Confidentiality	✓
Professional competence and due care	
Professional behaviour	
Objectivity	✓

Objectivity as V has a conflict of interest – which party are they representing?

Confidentiality as it would be very hard for V not use the knowledge they have for one company when arguing for the other's position.

151 Analyse S's dilemma from an ethical point of view.

The ethical principles involved here are as follows:

Integrity

S must be straightforward and honest in all professional and business relationships.

Integrity also implies fair dealing and truthfulness and there is a danger that the reference is not a fair or true representation of the facts as they sees them.

Objectivity

The large fee should not be allowed to colour S's judgement. This presents a self-interest threat.

It could also be argued that, because Kept Ltd is S's oldest client, then there is also a familiarity threat to objectivity.

Professional behaviour

Writing a reference that S suspects to be false could bring discredit to them and the profession.

ANSWERS TO PRACTICE QUESTIONS: SECTION 2

152 Comment on EACH of the ethical values suggested by the Marketing Director, highlighting the benefit of each, together with any reservations you may have concerning them.

1	All products should be purchased from local farms and suppliers where appropriate.
	This would have a positive impact from a sustainability perspective as it would reduce distribution miles and the associated impact on fossil fuels and pollution.
	The main reservation is the wording 'where appropriate' as there is no indication as to what 'appropriate' means – for example, Cosby could buy cheaper goods from overseas suppliers and argue that the low cost made it 'appropriate'.
2	All packing materials should be obtained from renewable sources where feasible.
	This would also have a positive impact from a sustainability perspective as it would reduce deforestation to provide cardboard and paper packaging.
	The main reservation is the wording 'where feasible' as there is no indication as to what 'feasible' means – for example, Cosby could buy cheaper goods with plastic packaging and argue that the low cost made it 'feasible'.
3	All suppliers to be paid on time.
	This should mean that suppliers are treated fairly. However, there is no indication that suppliers have any say in what constitutes 'on time'.
4	All suppliers to be paid fair prices as determined by the Purchasing Manager.
	This should also mean that suppliers are treated fairly.
	However, there is no indication that suppliers have any say in what constitutes 'fair prices' – the price needs to be seen to be reasonable and fair by both parties.

153 Identify which of the following are the most appropriate actions for J to take following the interview.

	Appropriate	Not appropriate
Because A shows business acumen, offer them the job.		✓
Because A has breached the fundamental principles of integrity and confidentiality, report them to the AAT.	✓	
Because A lacks integrity, inform them that they will not be offered the job.	✓	

J should not offer A the job because of a lack of integrity as indicated by A's willingness to breach confidentiality.

Furthermore, because A has breached the fundamental principles of integrity and confidentiality, J should report them to the AAT.

154 (i) Identify which type of threat this situation represents.

	✓
Self-interest threat	✓
Self-review threat	
Intimidation threat	
Advocacy threat	
Familiarity threat	

(ii) Identify what Jemalla's best course of action would be.

	✓
Continue as senior but make the partners aware of the inheritance	
Ask to be removed from the assignment	✓
Resign from Khan LLP	
Report the matter to the National Crime Agency (NCA)	

The best course of action is to remove Jemalla from this assurance engagement.

155 (i) Identify which type of threat this situation represents.

	✓
Self-interest threat	✓
Self-review threat	
Intimidation threat	
Advocacy threat	
Familiarity threat	

(ii) Suggest TWO safeguards the assurance firm should have in place concerning such a threat.

1	A policy requiring the immediate disclosure of such an offer of employment.
2	A policy requiring Suresh to be removed from the assurance engagement.

156 Explain whether G is allowed to use knowledge, information and experience gained from their previous employer in their new job.

> The key principle here is confidentiality.
>
> G is allowed to use general knowledge and experience from a previous employer but NOT specific information from that employer that is covered by the duty of confidentiality.
>
> This means that general accountancy, audit and management skills and knowledge can all be used but not specific information concerning Kirk Ltd.

ANSWERS TO PRACTICE QUESTIONS: SECTION 2

MONEY LAUNDERING

157 Identify which of the following are the most appropriate actions for Connor to take.

	Appropriate	Not appropriate
Continue with forging a relationship with the client in the usual manner.		✓
Inform the client that without knowing the correct address the client/accountant relationship cannot be forged.	✓	
Consider reporting the conversation to the National Crime Agency (NCA).	✓	

The reluctance to disclose an address raises concerns over possible money laundering.

Given this, as part of customer due diligence, the best course of action for Connor to take would be to inform the client that without knowing the correct address the client/accountant relationship cannot be forged.

Furthermore, Connor must consider reporting the conversation to the National Crime Agency (NCA).

158 (i) J decides to communicate this to the Finance Director of the client. What offence J will commit if they do this?

	✓
Breach of confidentiality	
Tipping off	✓
Money laundering	

(ii) What is the maximum sentence that J can receive if found guilty of the offence?

	✓
2 years	✓
5 years	
10 years	
14 years	

(iii) In the absence of an MLRO, who should J have approached with their concerns?

	✓
HMRC	
The National Crime Agency (NCA)	✓
The national press	

KAPLAN PUBLISHING 133

AAT: BUSINESS AWARENESS

159 Identify whether each of the following statements is TRUE or FALSE.

	True	False
Funds retained after discovery of a tax error amount to money laundering by Stoppard plc.	✓	
T should report the matter to the National Crime Agency (NCA).	✓	
T needs to make an authorised disclosure to the National Crime Agency NCA.	✓	

Funds dishonestly retained after discovery of a tax error become criminal property so their retention amounts to money laundering by Stoppard plc.

As T is now aware of the error, they should report to the National Crime Agency (NCA) that they suspect Stoppard plc of money laundering because it has refused to notify the matter to HMRC. T will be protected from a claim for breach of confidentiality when making this report.

Knowing they may have been involved in money laundering, T needs to make an authorised disclosure to NCA which may help protect T from a charge that they, in making the error, were engaged in money laundering.

160 Discuss whether or not LOFT and Co should agree to the payment.

> This scenario gives grounds for suspicion of money laundering.
>
> Why doesn't the client, H Ltd, simply want LOFT to repay them and then it up to them whether they want to pay anything to Q Ltd? Is it to make funds difficult to trace, so 'dirty cash' becomes a nice clean cheque from a reputable accounting firm?
>
> Any overpayment by a customer should be thoroughly investigated by a senior member of finance function staff and only repaid to the customer once it has been established that it is right/legal to do so.
>
> Similarly the request to pay a third party should be scrutinised before any payment is agreed to. Without further information the transaction does not make commercial sense.
>
> Unless investigations satisfy any concerns raised, then LOFT should refuse the payment and the MLRO should fill in a Suspicious Activity Report (SAR) to be sent to the NCA.

161 (a) Explain what Meera should do in response to the client's requests.

> **Fees**
>
> While some discounting of fees is seen as commercially acceptable way to win business, heavily discounted fees are perceived as a 'self-interest' threat to professional behaviour. This does not mean that they should be avoided at all costs but guidelines need to be followed.
>
> Fees should reflect the value of the professional services performed for the client and there is a risk with low fees of a perception that the quality of work could be impaired.
>
> **Tax bill**
>
> Meera should consider the fundamental principle of Integrity.
>
> It would be dishonest to promise to reduce a tax bill simply to gain a client when Meera believes the bill to be reasonable.

ANSWERS TO PRACTICE QUESTIONS: SECTION 2

(b) Should Meera tell HRMC about the error?

Meera should continue to advise Greg to contact the HMRC but it would be a breach of confidentiality to do so without Greg's express permission, which seems unlikely in this case.

(c) What should Meera do if Greg continues to refuse to inform the HMRC?

If Greg, after having had a reasonable time to reflect, does not correct the error, Meera should do the following:

- Inform Greg that the firm can no longer act on Greg's behalf because funds dishonestly retained after discovery of a tax error become criminal property so their retention amounts to money laundering.

- Make an internal report on the matter to the firm's MLRO.

162 (a) Explain what is meant by money laundering, the different categories of offence and possible punishments.

Money laundering is the process by which the proceeds of crime, either money or other property, are converted into assets, which appear to have a legitimate rather than an illegal origin. The aim of the process is to disguise the source of the property, in order to allow the holder to enjoy it free from suspicion as to its source.

The Proceeds of Crime Act 2002 (POCA) seeks to control money laundering by creating three categories of criminal offences in relation to the activity.

Laundering

Under the POCA, the three money laundering offences are

- Concealing – Concealing, disguising, converting, transferring or removing criminal property.

- Arranging – Taking part in an arrangement to facilitate the acquisition, use or control of criminal property.

- Acquisition – Acquiring, using or possessing criminal property.

These offences are punishable by a maximum of 14 years' imprisonment and/or a fine.

Failure to report

The second category of offence relates to failing to report a knowledge or suspicion of money laundering.

It is an offence for a person who knows or suspects that another person is engaged in money laundering not to report the fact to the appropriate authority. However, the offence only relates to individuals, such as accountants, who are acting in the course of business in the regulated sector.

The offences are punishable by a maximum of five years' imprisonment and/or a fine.

Tipping off

The third category of offence relates to tipping off. It is an offence to make a disclosure which is likely to prejudice any investigation under the Act.

The offences set out in these sections are punishable by a maximum of two years' imprisonment and/or a fine.

(b) Analyse the above scenario from the perspective of the law relating to money laundering. In particular, explain which criminal offences may have been committed by the various parties.

> K would be guilty of the primary offence of money laundering as explained in the section above.
>
> L is also guilty of an offence in relation to the Proceeds of Crime Act as they are clearly assisting K in the money laundering procedure. L is actively concealing and disguising criminal property, and the arrangement with K facilitates the retention of criminal property.
>
> M is equally guilty under the same provisions as L, in that they are actively engaged in the money laundering process, by producing false accounts.

TECHNOLOGY AFFECTING BUSINESS

TECHNOLOGY

163 How is the delivery of on-demand computing resources otherwise known?

	✓
Artificial Intelligence	
The Internet of things	
Big data	
Cloud computing	✓

By definition.

164 The process by which users log on to remote servers to access and process their files is best known as what?

	✓
Cloud computing	✓
Wide Area Network	
The internet	
Remote working	

This describes the basic idea of cloud computing.

ANSWERS TO PRACTICE QUESTIONS: SECTION 2

165 What are the TWO main types of cloud computing?

	✓
Public Cloud	✓
Restricted Cloud	
Private Cloud	✓
Amazon Cloud	

Public clouds are hosted by 3rd parties. Private clouds are managed over a private infrastructure.

166 Which THREE of the following are disadvantages of cloud computing?

	✓
Scalability	
Contract management	✓
Potential job losses	✓
Reliance on a third party	✓
Increases cost	
Reduced flexibility for employees	

The contract with the cloud provider will require careful management, this also increases reliance on the 3rd party and can result in job losses in IT support and maintenance roles.

Scalability, increased flexibility and reduced cost are all advantages of cloud computing.

167 Which THREE of the following are advantages of cloud computing?

	✓
Cost efficiency	✓
Scalability	✓
Flexibility	✓
Contract management	
Career opportunities	
Highlights inefficiencies	

Cloud technology allows pay as you go computing charged based on what a company actually needs and is therefore cost efficient.

Cloud computing allows frequent upgrades making it scalable.

Cloud computing supports remote working increasing flexibility.

AAT: BUSINESS AWARENESS

168 Which ONE of the following statements is true?

	✓
Process automation is only feasible for simple, repetitive tasks	
Process automation in complex business areas is beyond the limits of technology	
Process automation can enable a business to save costs	✓
Process automation usually leads to employee dissatisfaction	

Increasingly process automation is focussing on more complex business areas which can save costs and enable employees to focus on more value adding activities.

169 Machines working and reacting like human beings describes what?

	✓
Robotics	
Voice recognition	
Artificial intelligence	✓
The 4th Industrial Revolution	

This is a description of artificial intelligence.

170 Which of the following is a definition of a blockchain?

	✓
A technology that allows people who do not know each other to trust a shared record of events.	✓
A centralised, undistributed and private digital ledger that is used to record transactions.	
A sequence of transactions facilitated by the internet.	
A supply chain management system used to improve efficiency.	

By definition.

ANSWERS TO PRACTICE QUESTIONS: SECTION 2

171 Which THREE of the following statements about a blockchain are true?

	✓
Blockchain is regarded as a solution to cyber security risk	✓
Records in the blockchain are publically available and distributed across everyone that is part of the network of participants	✓
Records in the blockchain are always kept private to enhance security	
The verification of transactions is carried out by computers	✓
The verification of transaction is carried out by individuals	

In order to increase security and address the issue of cyber risk, all of the transactions in a blockchain are publically available and all transactions must be verified by a decentralised network of computers.

172 What is the internet of things?

	✓
An interactive collection of websites enabling users to communicate with one another.	
A technology that allows people who do not know each other to trust a shared record of event.	
Smart phones that enable users to control appliances within their home such as their heating or lighting.	
A network of smart devices with inbuilt software and connectivity which connect to the internet.	✓

By definition.

The third answer is too narrow an explanation although is an example of the use of the internet of things. The second statement is describing blockchain.

173 Advancements in mobile technology have contributed to the decline in the newspaper industry?

Is this statement true or false?

	✓
True	✓
False	

News is now consumed via mobile devices and is live rather than being a record of yesterday's news.

AAT: BUSINESS AWARENESS

174 Which THREE of the following are consequences of the developments in mobile technologies?

	✓
The decline of the newspaper industry	✓
The decline of social media interactions	
The decline in the number of retail bank branches	✓
An increase in the on demand nature of music	✓
An increase in the cost to manufacture smart devices	

Traditional industries such as banking and the news have now been replaced by online versions and apps. Music is also now being downloaded or streamed instantly.

Social media interactions have increased, and the costs have declined for manufacturers as the technologies develop.

175 Which ONE of the following tools will most help TPO achieve this goal?

	✓
Artificial intelligence	
Data analytics	✓
Process automation	
Data visualisation	

Data analytics can help an organisation analyse its customers into specific segments and understand more about their wants and needs.

Process automation is the use of technology to perform complex business processes. Artificial intelligence is where a machine can interpret and learn from external data such as voice recognition. Data visualisation is the displaying of complex data in a visually appealing and accessible way.

176 Which ONE of the following is a disadvantage of cloud computing?

	✓
Increased flexibility to working arrangements	
More reliance on third party suppliers	✓
Access to continually up to date software	
Easier integration of systems	

Many cloud services are provided by external third parties, and therefore reliance on these suppliers will be increased.

ANSWERS TO PRACTICE QUESTIONS: SECTION 2

177 Cloud computing enables multiple users to collaborate on a file at the same time, although this increases the risk of version control issues.

Is this statement true or false?

	✓
True	
False	✓

Multiple users can collaborate at the same time but cloud computing reduces the risk of version control issues.

178 Which THREE of the following are advantages of investing in process automation within the finance function?

	✓
Staff time can be freed up to focus on value adding activities	✓
No extra training will be required for staff as they will no longer be processing manually	
Staff will automatically buy in to having the mundane work taken from them	
Headcount reductions	✓
Improved efficiency	✓

Training (second answer) will still be required for staff to understand how the new software works and interfaces with their roles.

Process automation changes the way the finance function works and can lead to uncertainty around job security and future prospects, there will not necessarily be automatic buy in by the staff (third answer).

179 Which of the following statements regarding blockchain are true?

	✓
(i) and (ii)	
(i) and (iii)	✓
(iii) and (iv)	
(i), (ii) and (iii)	

Statements (i) and (iii) are true.

Statement (ii) is false because there is no agreement yet as to how these assets should be accounted for.

Statement (iv) is incorrect as cross border payments should be made much simpler through the use of blockchain.

AAT: BUSINESS AWARENESS

180 What type of technology are they making use of?

	✓
Social media	
Internet of things	
An intranet	
Mobile technology	✓

Use of mobile technology has reduced duplication and data entry. App software for logging and recording expenses has reduced manual processing, whilst delivering significant efficiencies and better quality management information.

DATA PROTECTION

181 Identify whether each of the following statements concerning principles within GDPR is TRUE or FALSE.

	True	False
Data must not be kept for longer than five years		✓
Data must be used for a specified, explicit purpose	✓	
Data held must be accurate	✓	
Data must be used transparently	✓	
Data should always be in a hard copy format		✓

GDPR requires data to be kept for no longer than is necessary, it does not suggest a number of years.

Data can be stored in a variety of formats and therefore the last statement is also incorrect.

182 Compliance with GDPR is the only thing that matters where data usage is concerned.

Is this statement TRUE or FALSE?

	✓
True	
False	✓

Compliance with legislation such as the GDPR laws is something that all companies should achieve. However, there are also ethical considerations concerning data, such as the principle of confidentiality, that need to be considered.

ANSWERS TO PRACTICE QUESTIONS: SECTION 2

183 Data Protection legislation, such as The Data Protection Act in the UK, typically focuses on which ONE of the following?

	✓
Issues concerning data held about incorporated entities	
Rights of the individual with regards to withholding information about oneself	
The way data about the individual is to be obtained, used and stored	✓
Aligning the information requirements between different countries	

The Act imposes obligations on the Data Controller (an individual or an organisation who has information about the individual), and the rights of the Data Subject (individual about whom the information is held).

184 Which of the following are typical rights of individuals with respect to data stored about them in data protection legislation?

	Yes	No
Right of subject access – individuals are entitled to be told whether the data controller holds personal data about them.	✓	
Right to prevent processing for the purposes of direct marketing.	✓	

185 In which of these scenarios would typical data protection legislation support Annan?

	✓
(i) only	
(ii) only	
Both	
Neither	✓

The credit file company must provide Annan with access to their credit file. However, Annan does not have the right to request this for free and may have to pay a fee.

Annan can also use typical data protection legislation to block direct marketing. However, junk mail is likely to be sent to a large number of recipients and therefore is not direct marketing.

INFORMATION-SECURITY AND CYBER-SECURITY

186 Which ONE of the following cyber-attacks does it appear that H Ltd was a victim of?

	✓
Keylogging	
Screenshotting	
Phishing	✓
Distributed denial of service	

It appears the manager has clicked on a link in a phishing email. Phishing involves using bogus emails to obtain security information and personal details.

Keylogging is where criminals record what the user types onto their keyboard.

A distributed denial of service attack is where multiple computers overwhelm a system with requests.

Screenshotting is not a type of attack.

187 Which type of cyber-attack involves criminals recording what a user types onto they keyboard?

	✓
Phishing	
Keylogging	✓
File hijacking	
Denial of service	

Keylogging is where criminals record what the user types onto their keyboard.

188 Which ONE of the following cyber-attacks does it appear that ABC Ltd was a victim of?

	✓
Phishing	✓
Keylogging	
File Hijacking	
Denial of service	

The use of emails to obtain bank information such as this is known as phishing.

ANSWERS TO PRACTICE QUESTIONS: SECTION 2

189 Which THREE of the following proposals would have an impact on the company's cyber-security risk?

	✓
Changing the specification of their best-selling product	
Acquiring a new manufacturing facility	✓
Revaluing non-current assets	
Outsourcing the Human Resources department	✓
Replacing laptops used by the sales force	✓

Acquiring a new facility will involve expanding the company's network.

Outsourcing the Human Resources department will mean allowing external access to employee data.

Replacing laptops will require secure disposal of the old machines (the new machines may well improve cyber-security if they run better protection software).

Changing the specification of a product and revaluing assets both involve altering information held by the company but not the potential access to it.

190 Based on the information provided, which ONE of the following features of FFK Company's business model is MOST likely to expose them to cyber-security threats?

	✓
Orders placed by phone	
Internal accounts department	
Use of a local courier service	
Inventory arrangement with component suppliers	✓

The link between the inventory store and the component suppliers expands FFK's network and so exposes them to a cyber-security threat.

Phone orders are a potential business risk but not a cyber-security threat.

AAT: BUSINESS AWARENESS

191 For each of the following scenarios, comment on whether it would impact cyber security risk:

Scenario	Comment
A business acquires a competitor.	An acquisition of a competitor is likely to lead to several IT challenges as systems are integrated. Any change like this could lead to increased opportunities for unauthorised access.
A large training organisation changes its organisational structure from divisional based on geography to a matrix structure.	A significant change in organisational restructure is likely to change reporting lines, and user access requirements. This could lead to potential cyber risks through inappropriate access to information or systems.
A local market trader decides who usually works Monday to Friday decides to open a stall at a new Sunday market.	No real impact on cyber-security risk. The local market trader has not had any significant change to operations, just effectively opening for longer hours.
A window cleaning business changes from accepting cash only to allowing customer to pay online.	The window cleaner has increased their usage of IT, so have potentially gone from very low likelihood of cyber security issues to significant risks relating to customers personal data.

192 Which TWO of the following would NOT be recommended to a business to help reduce cyber risks?

	✓
Regular IT training for staff	
Implementing access controls	
Ensure all staff to use the same memorable password so that people don't forget it	✓
Keeping software security up to date	
Establish and communicate IT policies and procedures	
Allowing all staff the freedom to use social media without any limitations to help motivate them	✓

All staff using the same password would be poor IT policy and increase the likelihood of both internal and external issues.

Allowing staff absolute freedom on social media could increase cyber risks through clicking on malicious links or falling for potential phishing attacks from hackers.

The rest are sensible precautions to help reduce the cyber risk an organisation faces.

ANSWERS TO PRACTICE QUESTIONS: SECTION 2

193 For each of the following statements, identify whether they should be included in an IT policy document advising on password security.

Statement	Included?
Use the same passwords for work and personal accounts, to make it easier for you to remember it	No
When the IT department ask for your password to work on your PC you must always give it to them	No
Keep a list of all your passwords either in your desk or another convenient location in case you forget them	No
Create strong passwords that are difficult to guess	Yes
Password321 is a stronger password than S9v£E1X	No

Creating a strong password that is difficult to guess is good general advice about passwords.

The rest are examples of bad password uses.

194 Identify whether each of the following statements given by the IT manager about why USB devices should be banned is TRUE or FALSE.

	True	False
USB drives could contain malware and when inserted into a network device, the malware could infect BUS Ltd systems.	✓	
Sensitive information could be stolen from BUS Ltd by employees using USB drives.	✓	
There are no controls that could protect sensitive information from being stolen on a USB drive.		✓
Antivirus software may not be able to prevent malware from a USB drive.	✓	
Employees losing USB drives containing sensitive information also presents a cyber-risk to BUS Ltd.	✓	

USB drives represent an additional endpoint on a network so increase cyber risk. Malware from the device is one of the risks, antivirus software could help with this, but may not be able to prevent all malware. Employees could transfer sensitive data onto the USB drives for work reasons and lose them, or they could steal sensitive information on a USB drive.

While there are controls, such as encryption, that could help reduce the threat from information theft, banning their use is also a control.

AAT: BUSINESS AWARENESS

195 Identify whether each of the following statements that were made at the meeting is TRUE or FALSE.

	True	False
Now our staff have been trained on email use and phishing, F&T Co will be protected from cyber-attacks as long as our staff do not open emails from senders they do not recognise		✓
We only need to worry about external threats to our IT systems		✓
The new antivirus software that we installed should help prevent our systems from being attacked	✓	
Paying someone to monitor the data moving across our network is a waste of resources and time		✓

Training is useful, but the staff still need to be vigilant for emails that look like they are from someone they trust but are not.

Internal threats may also be a problem – e.g. a disgruntled employee can often pose a significant cyber risk to a firm.

Antivirus software is a useful tool to help protect against cyber risks.

Monitoring network traffic can help identify attacks.

196 Which ONE of the following cyber-attacks does it appear that XYZ plc was a victim of?

	✓
Keylogging	
File hijacking	
Phishing	
Distributed denial of service	✓

Distributed denial of service (DDoS) attacks are used to bring down a business' website by overwhelming it with vast amounts of internet traffic.

INFORMATION AND BIG DATA

197 Which of the characteristics of good quality information is NOT being exhibited?

	✓
Understandable	
Complete	
Cost < benefit	✓
Accurate	

The information is taking 14 hours to gather which will cost money. If it is immediately being filed, the benefit will be less than this cost.

ANSWERS TO PRACTICE QUESTIONS: SECTION 2

198 In the context of data gathering and quality, which of the following statements are true?

	✓
(i) only	
(ii) only	✓
Both are true	
Neither are true	

Technology makes data gathering more efficient and quicker but the nature of the data is also changing, with more information than was previously available being gathered. For example, a customer may have considered alternatives before buying, in the past this fact would be lost. Short lead times enable business to respond to the signals data is revealing.

199 How are medium-term decisions better known?

	✓
Strategic	
Managerial	
Operational	
Tactical	✓

Tactical decisions are medium term and involve putting the strategic plan into action.

200 Which level of decision-making are they engaging in?

	✓
Strategic	✓
Tactical	
Acquisitional	
Operational	

Decisions about mergers and acquisitions happen at the strategic level.

201 Monitoring the performance of the machines enables which ONE of the following advantages specifically?

	✓
Forecasting	
Preventative maintenance	✓
Improved service for customers	
Supply chain collaboration	

Deviations from expected performance give early warning of potential problems and preventative maintenance can be scheduled at a convenient time and before an asset breaks down.

202 Which THREE of the following statements relating to big data are true?

	✓
Big data refers to any financial data over $1 billion	
The defining characteristics of big data are velocity, volume and variety	✓
Managing big data effectively can lead to increased competitive advantage	✓
The term big data means 'data that comes from many sources'	
Big data contains both financial and non-financial data	✓

Big data does not refer to any specific financial amount. Big data can indeed come from many sources, but this is too narrow a definition. Big data refers to the large volume of data, the many sources of data and the many types of data.

203 Assessing the reliability of big data refers to which of the 5 Vs?

	✓
Value	
Velocity	
Volume	
Visibility	
Veracity	✓

By definition. Veracity considers the reliability of the data being received.

204 Which of the 5 Vs of big data refers to the constant stream of data being produced?

	✓
Value	
Variety	
Veracity	
Volume	
Velocity	✓

By definition. The constant stream of data being produced in real time, is referred to as the velocity of big data.

ANSWERS TO PRACTICE QUESTIONS: SECTION 2

205 The need for systems to validate data links to which of the 5 Vs of big data?

	✓
Value	
Variety	
Veracity	✓
Volume	
Velocity	

Veracity relates to the extent that the data can be relied upon. Systems must ensure data can be validated to reduce uncertainty to tolerable levels.

206 In the world of big data and the role of accountants, which of the following statements are true?

	✓
(i) only	
(ii) only	✓
Both are true	
Neither are true	

There are many new possibilities for data analysis since there is also a change in the nature of the data. Statistical significance testing, for example, may become a required skill. Experts (data scientists) are becoming more common as a support to accountants.

207 (a) Identify the big data characteristic that matches each statement below.

Statement	Volume	Velocity	Variety	Veracity
FGH collects data from tens of thousands of customers each day, whether in stores or when logged into the website.	✓			
FGH compares data from different stores in order to assess whether or not identified trends are reliable.				✓
FGH uses extensive AI within a comprehensive data analytics system to analyse data obtained from loyalty cards in real time.		✓		
FGH collects data from all stores, of each type, from each country and from each customer type.			✓	

(b) Identify whether the following statements are TRUE or FALSE.

	True	False
Survey responses will be fully representative of customer attitudes and behaviours.		✓
Survey responses will be difficult to analyse due to the volume of data generated.		✓
Survey responses will be too detailed to be of any use for making strategic decisions.		✓

Survey responses may not be representative as (a) not all customers have loyalty cards, and (b) responses to surveys are not compulsory.

FGH has sophisticated systems designed to analyse the volume of data produced.

Even some strategic decision may be supported by such data – for example, if the majority of customers in a certain country give very negative feedback on FGH products, then the Board may decide to stop investing in the country concerned.

208 Which characteristic of Big Data may be missing from Sara's data?

	✓
Value	
Variety	
Veracity	✓
Volume	
Velocity	

Veracity refers to the accuracy and truthfulness of the data. If this is missing, it can lead to inaccurate conclusions being drawn.

209 Identify whether the following statements are TRUE or FALSE.

	True	False
Use of Big Data can reduce costs.	✓	
Use of Big Data can reduce waiting times.	✓	
The use of Big Data in healthcare poses new ethical and legal challenges.	✓	

Big Data can result in cost savings for many reasons including greater efficiency, better planning and so on.

For example, predictive analytics can assist with staffing by predicting admission rates over a period of two weeks, say, which will allow the hospital to better allocate staff based on need. This reduces overstaffing issues, increases hospital efficiency, and thus reduces costs.

Furthermore, such predictive analysis would also decrease patient wait times.

The use of Big Data in healthcare poses new ethical and legal challenges because of the personal nature of the information enclosed. Ethical and legal challenges include the risk to compromise privacy and personal autonomy.

ANSWERS TO PRACTICE QUESTIONS: SECTION 2

COMMUNICATING INFORMATION

VISUALISING AND COMMUNICATING INFORMATION

210 The use of a dashboard to present data is an example of what?

	✓
Data visualisation	✓
Data simplification	
Graphical data	
Information processing	

Data visualisation is an enabling technology that complements data analytics by facilitating user friendly and accessible presentation of key data.

211 The provision of information in a more appealing and understandable manner is often referred to as what?

	✓
Artificial Intelligence	
Data simplification	
Cloud computing	
Data visualisation	✓

By definition.

212 Which of the following is not necessarily a benefit of data visualisation?

	✓
Improves the accuracy of the data being analysed	✓
Problem areas can be identified sooner	
Understandable by many users	
Supports prompt decision making	

AAT: BUSINESS AWARENESS

213 Which of the following statements about data visualisation is true?

	✓
The most common use of data visualisation is the creation of a dashboard displaying real time KPIs.	✓
Data is always displayed in standardised formats to ensure consistency.	
Data visualisation refers to data that is analysed using virtual reality software.	
Increased use of data visualisation within organisations increases the need for more IT experts.	

The graphic produced will only be as accurate as the original data. Visualisation does not improve this accuracy.

214 ELC Co has produced some infographics to enable the visualisation of its sales data.

Which THREE of the following characteristics will make the infographics more effective?

	✓
Details of sales made to each customer on a daily basis	
The ability to drill down to obtain further detail	✓
Avoidance of technical jargon	✓
Access granted to all sales staff	
Intuitive visualisations needing little explanation	✓

The detail described in the first answer is too detailed for the infographic.

Access will not necessarily be suitable for all sales staff as described in the fourth answer.

215 Directors will be the stakeholder of the finance function most likely to require data visualisation.

Is this statement true or false?

	✓
True	
False	✓

The directors seek insight and clarity from information provided by finance, and this is often required in the form of data visualisation. However, all stakeholders may use data visualisation, just for different reasons.

ANSWERS TO PRACTICE QUESTIONS: **SECTION 2**

216 **Which of the following statements is the least appropriate method of dealing with this problem?**

	✓
Highlight and explain any unusual items in the report	
Discuss with users the most appropriate form of report	
Include clear graphics and charts, and ensure that the narrative is as simple as possible	
Ensure that only individuals with some accounting knowledge are appointed to management positions	✓
Highlight and explain any unusual items in the report	

Management accounting reports should be understandable by non-financial managers. It is totally misguided to think that all managers should be financially literate, and it is important to make sure that reports to non-financial managers are clear and well presented, and that difficult or unusual issues are explained carefully.

217 **Which of the following charts or diagrams would be most suitable for showing this information?**

	✓
Pie chart	
Component bar chart	✓
Simple bar chart	
Multiple bar chart	

A component bar chart shows the total sales in any one year. The individual components of each bar should show the sales for the three different products.

218 **XYZ produces three main products. Which would be the most appropriate chart or diagram for showing total turnover and its product analysis month by month?**

	✓
Area chart	
Line graph	
Pie chart	
Component bar chart	✓

A bar chart is a good way of illustrating total sales month by month. The length of the bar each month is a measure of total sales. The bar can be divided into three parts, to show the amount of sales achieved for each of the three products. This is called a component bar chart.

KAPLAN PUBLISHING

219 What would be the most effective way of demonstrating a trend in new mobile telephone sales from January to December 20X1?

	✓
Pie chart	
Bar chart	
Table	
Line graph	✓

Line graphs are very useful to demonstrate trends.

220 Which of the following graphs would best be used to provide exact data?

	✓
Pie chart	
Bar chart	
Table	✓
Line graph	

Tables are best when exact data is required. Detail is lost when charts and graphs are used.

221 Which member of the sales team had the highest sales in February?

	✓
Jenny Manku	
Roger Perwaiz	
Mike Capstick	
Sharon Newt	✓

222 Referring to the graph which statements are true and which are false?

	True	False
Area 3 shows the best performance in Q3	✓	
Area 2 sales are consistent quarter on quarter		✓
Q4 has the largest volume of sales across all areas	✓	
Area 1 shows the best performance in Q2	✓	

ANSWERS TO PRACTICE QUESTIONS: **SECTION 2**

223 Explain the benefits of such dashboards.

Dashboards are very good at the following

- Giving a summary of the current position of the business.
- Showing an overview of the business performance.
- Highlighting areas of concern for further investigation.

The use of graphs and visualisations has increased as they have the following benefits:

- Many users find it easier to interpret visual data than tables of figures.
- A range of charts and diagrams enables the user to see the bigger picture.
- It may be easier to identify patterns and trends in data by using a range of charts and diagrams.
- It may be easier to identify interrelationships in data.

224 Explain the performance of the chocolate unicorn over the period concerned.

January to April

- Both revenue and volume increased from January to April, reflecting increasing demand.
- This is probably due to increasing awareness by customers as the product was only introduced in January.
- Sales may also have increased in the run up to religious holidays, such as Easter.
- The fact that both revenue and volume increased at a similar rate would also suggest that average selling prices were pretty constant.

April to June

- In May volumes increased more quickly than previously, presumably as a result of winning the supermarket contract.
- However, sales revenue fell during the same period, which can only be explained if average prices fell significantly.
- It may be that Higgs and Co had to offer the chocolate unicorn at a significant discount to the supermarket chain to win the contract. This may be because the supermarket chain wanted a high mark-up and exercised their power over Higgs and Co, or because they wanted to release the new product at an introductory low price and put pressure on Higgs and Co to enable this.
- However, even a low price to supermarkets would not explain overall revenue falling unless sales through other channels were lower as well, either because customers bought from the cheaper supermarket (i.e. the supermarket sales displaced other sales) or because other retailers put pressure on Higgs and Co to drop their prices to them as well.

AAT: BUSINESS AWARENESS

225 (a) Using the data provided, identify on FOUR key findings relating to the performance of Hus Ltd, and explain a possible reason for each finding. Focus on both the performance of the company as a whole, and each product line.

Sales have been increasing year on year between 20X2 to 20X4.

- This has been mainly due to the introduction of the new camera product line in 20X3, which continued to grow in 20X4.

The lights product has seen a high number of returns and complaints this year.

- The issue is likely to be as a result of insufficient supervisor resource on the lights production line. This may be harming the quality of the product, leading to more complaints and returns, and the reduced review scores as shown in the retailer website review score data.

The Lights product has seen a decline in sales levels in 20X4.

- The poor review scores due to the quality issues mentioned above will be leading customers to look elsewhere in the highly competitive environment. Customers will switch to Drench or Smarty as both now have higher scores for their lighting products, with Smarty likely to be cheaper, too.

Consistent growth from 20X2 to 20X4 for the core doorbell product.

- This is particularly impressive given the competition in the market, and is likely due to the strong reputation and brand name that Hus Ltd has developed in becoming the leading producer of doorbells.

(b) Identify TWO pieces of additional information that could improve your analysis.

Possible answers include:

- Prior year figures for complaints and returns
- Review scores on online retailer website for doorbells and cameras
- Sales information of competitors to allow for a comparison

Section 3

MOCK ASSESSMENT QUESTIONS

TASK 1 (20 MARKS)

This task is about organisations and ethics for accountants.

(a) Identify whether each of the following statements is TRUE or FALSE. **(2 marks)**

	True	False
Limited companies are owned by individual people, trusts, associations and/or other companies.		
Wages paid to the owner of a sole trader business are considered to be normal business expenses.		

(b) (i) Identify which ONE of the following structures is suited to an organisation which wants to achieve standardisation and economies of scale. **(1 mark)**

	✓
Functional	
Divisional	
Matrix	

(ii) Identify which type of control is described by each of the following statements.

(3 marks)

Statement	Centralised control	Decentralised control	Wide span of control	Narrow span of control
The manager has a small number of employees under their direct control.				
Decision making and control is managed by the main board of directors and not delegated.				
The organisation has high flexibility but a lower level of control.				

AAT: **BUSINESS AWARENESS**

Great Gears Limited manufactures and sells gearboxes in the automotive industry. The company was set up fifty years ago and many of its processes are very labour-intensive and inefficient. This has meant that the company is now struggling to be cost competitive and the board are considering introducing high levels of automation and robotics to improve quality and reduce cost. Automation would result in extensive redundancies. The company has no official trade union.

(c) (i) For each of the stakeholder groups listed below, identify whether they have high or low interest, and high or low power. **(3 marks)**

	Interest		Power	
	Low	High	Low	High
Production employees				
Local shops				
Suppliers of parts				

(ii) Complete the following statement about a company's board of directors by selecting ONE option. **(1 mark)**

Directors have a duty to _____.

Options	✓
ensure all shareholders are happy	
promote the success of the company	
recruit new directors	

Maria is an accountant in industry. Maria has been investigating the company's expenses system and has found some errors where senior staff are claiming, and getting paid, expenses that do not comply with the company's policies on expenses. Maria raised this with the manager of the finance department, Ellie, who said to sign off the investigation as 'satisfactory' or else Maria's career in the company would be in doubt.

(d) (i) Identify how Maria's principles are threatened by completing the following statement. **(2 marks)**

This is...	**Gap 1**	...threat to...	**Gap 2**

Gap 1 options	✓
an advocacy	
a self-review	
an intimidation	

Gap 2 options	✓
objectivity	
confidentiality	
professional competence and due care	

Accountants in the UK are required to keep their knowledge up to date, and to undertake continuing professional development (CPD).

(ii) Identify which ONE of the following fundamental principles this protects. **(1 mark)**

	✓
Integrity	
Objectivity	
Professional competence and due care	
Professional behaviour	

(iii) Identify which TWO of the following are advantages of a rules-based approach to ethics over a principles-based approach to ethics. **(2 marks)**

	✓
Easy enforcement	
Applicable to all situations	
Reduced misunderstandings or misinterpretation	
Less chance of people finding loopholes	

(e) (i) For each statement below, identify the safeguard needed to protect professional ethics. **(3 marks)**

Statement	Disciplinary procedures	Membership of professional body and CPD	A well-publicised complaints system
There are poor payroll controls in place which could result in staff claiming excessive expenses.			
With global developments over data protection, there is a risk that accountants' knowledge may be out of date.			
In order to reduce costs (and fees), an accountancy firm uses unqualified staff to carry out roles that qualified staff should undertake at a client.			

(ii) In which TWO of the following situations can an accountant in practice disclose confidential information about a client without the client's express permission?

(2 marks)

	✓
Information concerning historical losses has been requested verbally by the relevant tax authority.	
Information has been requested by officers of the NCA investigating money laundering.	
Disclosure is required to comply with the practice's internal policy.	
There is a professional duty to disclose due to the public interest.	

TASK 2 (18 MARKS)

This task is about analysing the external environment.

> Eco-shoes Limited manufactures and sells sports footwear made using natural and recycled materials. Sales are made through the company's own retail stores in major cities, via its website and through a mobile app. Raw materials are imported from South America and Asia but all sales are currently just within the UK.
>
> The company has seen high growth over the last five years, has built a strong brand and can charge higher than average prices for its shoes. Shoes are mainly bought by young professionals, mostly because of the environmental credentials but also because the shoes are currently seen as 'cool'.

(a) (i) For each of the three specified PESTLE categories (Economic, Social, Technological) identify ONE threat facing Eco-shoes. **(3 marks)**

 (ii) Explain ONE action Eco-shoes could take to reduce threats under each category. **(6 marks)**

	Threat	Action to reduce threat
Economic		
Social		

MOCK ASSESSMENT QUESTIONS: **SECTION 3**

Technological		

(iii) Identify ONE of the remaining PESTLE categories. **(1 mark)**

(b) Match each of the technologies to ONE significant advantage it brings to accounting systems used in business. **(4 marks)**

Technology	Frees up time for more valuable work	Enhanced performance appraisal	Security and confidentiality	Speeds up data entry
Artificial intelligence				
Data visualisation				
Electronic document filing				
Process automation				

(c) (i) Identify whether each of the following statements about the financial statements of limited companies is TRUE or FALSE. **(2 marks)**

	True	False
The term "true and fair" is precisely defined in UK company law.		
Financial statements must be approved by all shareholders.		

KAPLAN PUBLISHING

(ii) Complete each of the following definitions about unlimited liability partnerships by selecting ONE option. **(2 marks)**

| The profit share ratio (PSR) is defined by: | Gap 1 | Goodwill in a partnership can be defined as: | Gap 2 |

Gap 1 options	✓
the partnership agreement.	
the partnership contract.	
the amount by which the business's total value exceeds the value of its separately identifiable net assets.	
accumulated profits made by the partnership.	

Gap 2 options	✓
the partnership agreement.	
the partnership contract.	
the amount by which the business's total value exceeds the value of its separately identifiable net assets.	
accumulated profits made by the partnership.	

TASK 3 (17 MARKS)

(a) (i) Identify which ONE of the following is NOT a feature of blockchains. **(1 mark)**

	✓
Transactions are recorded by all parties who make up the chain	
Cryptographic hashes ensure chains cannot be broken	
A single entity can add new blocks without verification	
Central authorities, such as government departments, cannot interfere with blockchains	

(ii) Identify which TWO of the following are benefits of blockchain. **(2 marks)**

	✓
Simplified financial reporting	
Can be used for non-financial data as well as financial transactions	
Eco-friendly	
Security	

(b) Complete each of the following definitions about cloud accounting by selecting ONE of the following options for each gap. **(2 marks)**

Cloud computing allows frequent upgrades making it – **GAP 1**.

Cloud technology allows 'pay as you go' computing charged based on what a company actually needs and is therefore – **GAP 2**.

Gap 1 options	✓
more cost efficient	
more controllable	
more scalable	

Gap 2 options	✓
more cost efficient	
more controllable	
more scalable	

(c) Identify which TWO of the following proposals are most likely to result in an increase in cyber-security risks. **(2 marks)**

	✓
Introducing cloud accounting	
Outsourcing some processes within the finance function	
Changing the depreciation policy on plant and equipment	
Offering a price discount on old inventory	

(d) Identify whether each of the following statements about data protection legislation is TRUE or FALSE. **(4 marks)**

	True	False
GDPR requires personal data to be deleted after three years.		
Personal data shall be adequate, relevant and not excessive in relation to the purpose or purposes for which they are processed.		
Individuals have the right to stop companies processing their data for marketing purposes.		
Under GDPR the maximum possible fine is 20 million Euros.		

(e) Identify which quality of a service is described in each of the following statements.

(4 marks)

	Intangibility	Inseparability	Variability	Perishability
It is hard to assess the quality of a service in advance				
Services cannot be stored for sale in the future				
The quality of a service depends on who delivers it				
It is hard to separate provision and consumption of a service				

Glau Ltd is expanding and needs to hold higher inventory levels, and are considering how they should fund the extra investment required.

(f) Identify the funding source that each of the following statements relates to. **(2 marks)**

Statement	Working Capital	Loan	Equity
Glau Ltd could consider cutting the dividend.			
Most suitable for short term funding of inventory.			

TASK 4 (10 MARKS)

This task is about ethical and legal compliance.

B has recently been appointed as a senior manager of a small accountancy partnership. The other senior managers are very pleased with B's appointment as the firm has really struggled to attract, recruit and retain good staff.

At the last meeting of the partners it was decided that the remuneration and benefits package for senior staff (including senior managers) was no longer competitive and that it needed revising.

B was asked to draw up the new package and, after considerable research and benchmarking, has decided that a significant increase is needed in the benefits package.

(a) (i) Discuss which ethical principles are potentially compromised here. **(4 marks)**

(ii) Explain what steps B should take in response to the threats identified above.

(4 marks)

(b) D works as a credit controller in the Finance department of Sansom Ltd. During D's lunch in the staff café, they overheard a conversation that suggested that someone had made a suspicious activity report to the firm's MLRO.

After lunch D went straight to the Finance Director, E, to ask if they knew anything about this.

(i) What offence has D potentially committed? **(1 mark)**

	✓
Breach of confidentiality	
Tipping off	
Money laundering	
Layering	

(ii) What is the maximum prison sentence that D can receive if found guilty of the offence? **(1 mark)**

	✓
2 years	
3 years	
10 years	
14 years	

TASK 5 (10 MARKS)

This task is about the microeconomic environment and sustainability.

(a) (i) Identify which TWO of the following events will cause a shift in the supply curve of a normal good. **(2 marks)**

	✓
A change in the price charged	
A change in consumer incomes	
A change in government subsidies	
A change in raw material costs	

A normal good, called N, has a substitute, called S. The price of S has increased.

(ii) Identify the effect of the rise in the price of S on the quantity demanded of N, as shown on its demand curve. Select ONE option. **(1 mark)**

	✓
There will be a movement down the demand curve	
The demand curve will shift to the right	
The demand curve will shift to the left	
There will be a movement up the demand curve	

Highfashion plc, a national chain of high street fashion clothing retailers, has recently got into financial problems and has been bought out by, Buyme plc, a large online retailer, who plans to close all high street stores but retain the Highfashion brand.

(iii) Identify which TWO of the following will be the impact of the collapse and subsequent purchase of Highfashion plc. **(2 marks)**

	✓
Lower prices for high street fashion clothing as a result of reduced competition due to fewer participants.	
Heavy discounting from other online fashion retailers as a competitive response to protect their market share.	
Potentially unethical behaviour as other fashion retailers respond by putting more pressure on suppliers to cut prices.	
Increased market share for other online fashion retailers, which will lead to increased economies of scale.	

(b) (i) Complete the following statement about the meaning of sustainability by selecting ONE option. **(1 mark)**

A sustainable business _____, without compromising the ability of future generations to meet their own needs.

Options	✓
aims to grow is a consistent manner	
aims to reduce its carbon footprint	
meets the needs of the present	

(ii) Identify ONE type of sustainability that each of the following stated organisational policies relates to. **(3 marks)**

	Social sustainability	Environmental sustainability	Financial sustainability
"Use offsetting schemes to compensate for emission of greenhouse gases (e.g. schemes to plant additional trees somewhere else)."			
"Pay taxes without finding loopholes to avoid them."			
"Invest in people over the long term by fostering diversity, providing challenging and exciting work and development opportunities, and rewarding for performance."			

(iii) Identify whether the following statement is TRUE or FALSE. **(1 mark)**

	True	False
Trying to achieve better sustainability will inevitably increase costs and reduce profits.		

AAT: BUSINESS AWARENESS

TASK 6 (13 MARKS)

This task is about communication and visualisation.

Today's date is 1 July 20X2. You work for Noble Nosh Ltd, a chain of high-quality restaurants.

- Noble Nosh Ltd is owned by friends Sam Selmer and Juliana Cortez. Sam is a top chef and Juliana a wine expert. The first restaurant was opened in London three years ago. A major emphasis of the restaurants is in offering a rich fusion of world foods, using high quality organic ingredients and careful matching of wines to foods.
- The customer base is expanding, as the quality of the food and drinks have received rave reviews in newspapers and lifestyle magazines, as well as online. The company has continued to expand and now has three restaurants in the greater London area. The last restaurant, C, was opened in March.
- Each restaurant has its own head chef and other key staff, although menus are set by Sam and Juliana. Eight further staff are employed at head office.
- Noble Nosh Ltd's suppliers typically allow a 60-day payment term.

A performance dashboard has been provided for the six-month period to 30 June 20X2.

The Finance Manager is responsible for analysing results for use by Sam and Juliana and other managers in the business. Unfortunately, the Finance Manager is currently ill.

Sam and Juliana have asked you to help with this analysis in the absence of the Finance Manager. They would like to know about:

- the performance of the business over the six months to 30 June 20X2
- the expected performance of the business for the next six months
- any additional information that it would be useful to have on the dashboard.

(a) Prepare a response to Sam and Juliana in which you:

(i) Discuss the performance of the business over the six months to 30 June 20X2 and the expected performance of the business for the next six months. **(11 marks)**

(ii) Identify TWO pieces of additional information which would be useful to show on the performance dashboard. **(2 marks)**

Task 6: Dashboard

Number of customers						
Restaurant	Jan	Feb	Mar	Apr	May	Jun
A	1,500	1,550	1,580	1,625	1,700	1,710
B	620	625	480	490	520	540
C	0	0	450	600	680	700
Total	2,120	2,175	2,510	2,715	2,900	2,950

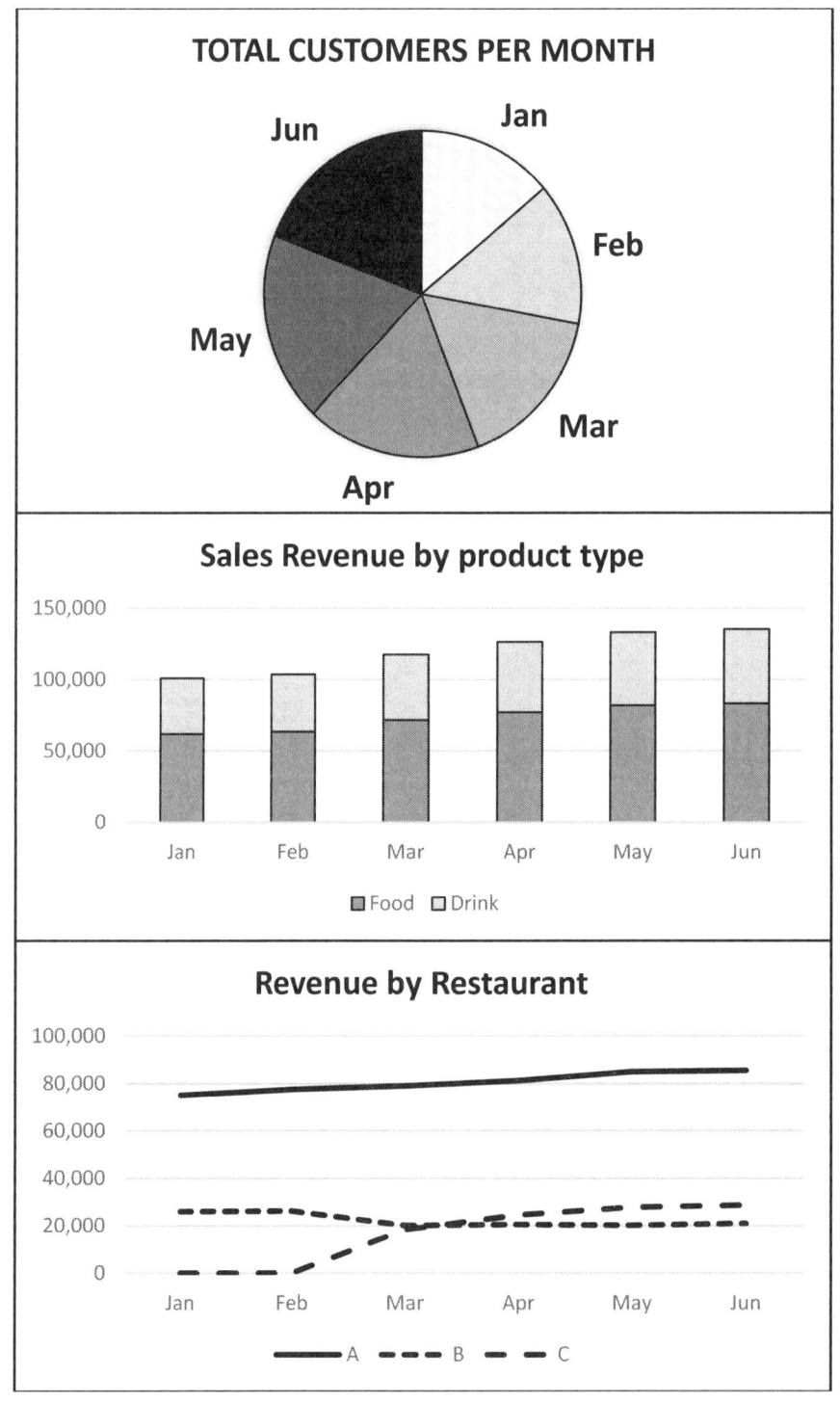

TASK 7 (12 MARKS)

This task is about risk and big data.

(a) Identify ONE appropriate strategy to deal with each of the following risks. **(2 marks)**

	Transfer	Accept	Reduce	Avoid
An open air music festival organiser is concerned about how global warming may affect the weather.				
A package holiday operator is concerned about the high possibility of a civil war in country A.				

(b) Identify which ONE of the following factors would normally be classed as a strategic risk.

(1 mark)

	✓
Possible obsolescence of slow moving inventory	
Problems recruiting delivery drivers	
A worldwide ban on the use of a key chemical on health grounds	
A minor customer going bankrupt	

Hidden Kingdom plc operates a number of theme parts and amusement arcades across the UK. The company collects data from the following sources:

- Ticket purchases, including price and date of entry, on the company website and on site
- Customer arrival and exit times
- Shop and restaurant sales on site
- Customer feedback surveys
- Customer loyalty cards
- Website activity
- Social media activity.

(c) (i) Identify which TWO of the following are benefits for Hidden Kingdom plc of having the data on ticket purchases. **(2 marks)**

	✓
Enables better staff scheduling	
Provides Hidden Kingdom with a range of secondary data for research	
Simplifies Hidden Kingdom's tills and operating systems	
Enables more targeted marketing efforts	

(ii) Identify the big data characteristic that underlies the challenge or benefit for Hidden Kingdom described in each statement below. **(3 marks)**

Statement	Volume	Velocity	Variety	Veracity
Data derived from shops separates out sales of 500 different products, matched to 25 shops, 125 different members of staff and the day and time of day the sales were made.				
Hidden Kingdom collects and processes data from over 4 million visitors each year and monitors their activities every minute they are in the theme parks.				
The on-site shop and restaurant data collection is deemed to be accurate as it is decided by and controlled by Hidden Kingdom in the systems they use.				

(iii) Complete the following statement about decision making by selecting ONE option. **(1 mark)**

This information will assist in making decisions about which dates to open which theme parks, so it is an example of _____ decision.

Options	✓
a strategic	
a managerial	
an operational	

(iv) Identify whether the following statement about the quality of the information is TRUE or FALSE. **(1 mark)**

	True	False
The information derived from social media is likely to be more reliable than that obtained from shop sales for estimating future demand.		

Hidden Kingdom's Finance function interacts with other business functions, for example, the Human Resources function and the Operations function.

(d) Identify which TWO pieces of information Hidden Kingdom's Finance function would directly receive from the Park Operations function, not from the Human Resources function. **(2 marks)**

	✓
Ride maintenance engineer pay rise	
Overtime hours worked this week by shop staff due to sickness	
Changes in overtime policy for peak holiday periods	
Travel expenses due for reimbursement to safety inspectors	

Section 4

ANSWERS TO MOCK ASSESSMENT QUESTIONS

TASK 1 (20 MARKS)

(a) Identify whether each of the following statements is TRUE or FALSE. (2 marks)

	True	False
Limited companies are owned by individual people, trusts, associations and/or other companies.	✓	
Wages paid to the owner of a sole trader business are considered to be normal business expenses.		✓ they would be drawings

(b) (i) Identify which ONE of the following structures is suited to an organisation which wants to achieve standardisation and economies of scale. (1 mark)

	✓
Functional	✓
Divisional	
Matrix	

(ii) Identify which type of control is described by each of the following statements. (3 marks)

Statement	Centralised control	Decentralised control	Wide span of control	Narrow span of control
The manager has a small number of employees under their direct control.				✓
Decision making and control is managed by the main board of directors and not delegated.	✓			
The organisation has high flexibility but a lower level of control.		✓		

KAPLAN PUBLISHING

(c) (i) For each of the stakeholder groups listed below, identify whether they have high or low interest, and high or low power. **(3 marks)**

	Interest		Power	
	Low	High	Low	High
Production employees		✓	✓	
Local shops		✓	✓	
Suppliers of parts	✓		✓	

> **Note**:
>
> The workforce will have high interest as their jobs are threatened but would have little collective power.
>
> Local shops would be very interested in the decision as they probably rely on employees at the factory spending money in their shops. However, they have little influence over the decision.
>
> Suppliers will not be interested in how the gearboxes are made, as long as the factory continues to operate. They will have little power to influence the decision.

(ii) Complete the following statement about a company's board of directors by selecting ONE option. **(1 mark)**

Directors have a duty to _____.

Options	✓
ensure all shareholders are happy	
promote the success of the company	✓
recruit new directors	

(d) (i) Identify how Maria's principles are threatened by completing the following statement. **(2 marks)**

This is...	Gap 1	...threat to...	Gap 2

Gap 1 options	✓
an advocacy	
a self-review	
an intimidation	✓

Gap 2 options	✓
objectivity	✓
confidentiality	
professional competence and due care	

(ii) Identify which ONE of the following fundamental principles this protects. **(1 mark)**

	✓
Integrity	
Objectivity	
Professional competence and due care	✓
Professional behaviour	

ANSWERS TO MOCK ASSESSMENT QUESTIONS: SECTION 4

(iii) Identify which TWO of the following are advantages of a rules-based approach to ethics over a principles-based approach to ethics. **(2 marks)**

	✓
Easy enforcement	✓
Applicable to all situations	
Reduced misunderstandings or misinterpretation	✓
Less chance of people finding loopholes	

(e) (i) For each statement below, identify the safeguard needed to protect professional ethics. **(3 marks)**

Statement	Disciplinary procedures	Membership of professional body and CPD	A well-publicised complaints system
There are poor payroll controls in place which could result in staff claiming excessive expenses.	✓		
With global developments over data protection, there is a risk that accountants' knowledge may be out of date.		✓	
In order to reduce costs (and fees), an accountancy firm uses unqualified staff to carry out roles that qualified staff should undertake at a client.			✓

(ii) In which TWO of the following situations can an accountant in practice disclose confidential information about a client without the client's express permission? **(2 marks)**

	✓
Information concerning historical losses has been requested verbally by the relevant tax authority.	
Information has been requested by officers of the NCA investigating money laundering.	✓
Disclosure is required to comply with the practice's internal policy.	
There is a professional duty to disclose due to the public interest.	✓

KAPLAN PUBLISHING

AAT: BUSINESS AWARENESS

TASK 2 (18 MARKS)

(a) (i) For each of the three specified PESTLE categories (Economic, Social, Technological) identify ONE threat facing Eco-Shoes. **(3 marks)**

(ii) Explain ONE action Eco-Shoes could take to reduce threats under each category.
(6 marks)

Note: only one threat needs to be identified for each and one recommendation for EST categories.

	Threat	Action to reduce threat
Economic	An economic downturn could reduce disposable income and therefore lower demand for expensive footwear. (1 mark) Changes in exchange rates could increase the cost of raw materials, thus reducing margins. (1 mark)	Offer a range of cheaper footwear (1 mark) and loyalty discounts to enable customers to afford the shoes. (1 mark) Increase range of sales locations (1 mark) for example other locations outside of UK. (1 mark)
Social	Changes in fashion may mean the designs are no longer seen as 'cool' thus reducing demand. (1 mark)	Increase investment in designers and market research (1 mark) to ensure new designs target to changes in fashion. (1 mark) Reduce length of supply chains (1 mark) to ensure new products can be developed quickly.
Technological	Cyber-security risks where hackers try to disable the website, such as through a DOS attack. (1 mark) Mobile app may not be compatible with all new phones, thus frustrating richer potential customers. (1 mark)	Invest in cyber-security systems disaster recovery (1 mark) to ensure website can be up and running again quickly. Invest in app updates (1 mark) to ensure all major platforms are compatible. (1 mark)

(iii) Identify ONE of the remaining PESTLE categories. **(1 mark)**

Political
Environmental
Legal

ANSWERS TO MOCK ASSESSMENT QUESTIONS: SECTION 4

(b) Match each of the technologies to ONE significant advantage it brings to accounting systems used in business. **(4 marks)**

Technology	Frees up time for more valuable work	Enhanced performance appraisal	Security and confidentiality	Speeds up data entry
Artificial intelligence				✓
Data visualisation		✓		
Electronic document filing			✓	
Process automation	✓			

(c) (i) Identify whether each of the following statements about the financial statements of limited companies is TRUE or FALSE. **(2 marks)**

	True	False
The term "true and fair" is precisely defined in UK company law.		✓
Financial statements must be approved by all shareholders.		✓ Not 'all'.

(ii) Complete each of the following definitions about unlimited liability partnerships by selecting ONE option. **(2 marks)**

The profit share ratio (PSR) is defined by:	Gap 1	Goodwill in a partnership can be defined as:	Gap 2

Gap 1 options	✓
the partnership agreement.	✓
the partnership contract.	
the amount by which the business's total value exceeds the value of its separately identifiable net assets.	
accumulated profits made by the partnership.	

Gap 2 options	✓
the partnership agreement.	
the partnership contract.	
the amount by which the business's total value exceeds the value of its separately identifiable net assets.	✓
accumulated profits made by the partnership.	

TASK 3 (17 MARKS)

(a) (i) Identify which ONE of the following is NOT a feature of blockchains. **(1 mark)**

	✓
Transactions are recorded by all parties who make up the chain	
Cryptographic hashes ensure chains cannot be broken	
A single entity can add new blocks without verification	✓
Central authorities, such as government departments, cannot interfere with blockchains	

(ii) Identify which TWO of the following are benefits of blockchains. **(2 marks)**

	✓
Simplified financial reporting	
Can be used for non-financial data as well as financial transactions	✓
Eco-friendly	
Security	✓

(b) Complete each of the following definitions about cloud accounting by selecting ONE of the following options for each gap. **(2 marks)**

Cloud computing allows frequent upgrades making it – **GAP 1**.

Cloud technology allows 'pay as you go' computing charged based on what a company actually needs and is therefore – **GAP 2**.

Gap 1 options	✓
more cost efficient	
more controllable	
more scalable	✓

Gap 2 options	✓
more cost efficient	✓
more controllable	
more scalable	

(c) Identify which TWO of the following proposals are most likely to result in an increase in cyber-security risks. **(2 marks)**

	✓
Introducing cloud accounting	✓
Outsourcing some processes within the finance function	✓
Changing the depreciation policy on plant and equipment	
Offering a price discount on old inventory	

Cloud accounting could increase risk due to many employees accessing company data via mobile devices.

Outsourcing some accounting processes will mean allowing external access to company data.

ANSWERS TO MOCK ASSESSMENT QUESTIONS: **SECTION 4**

(d) Identify whether each of the following statements about data protection legislation is TRUE or FALSE. **(4 marks)**

	True	False
GDPR requires personal data to be deleted after three years.		✓
Personal data shall be adequate, relevant and not excessive in relation to the purpose or purposes for which they are processed.	✓	
Individuals have the right to stop companies processing their data for marketing purposes.	✓	
Under GDPR the maximum possible fine is 20 million Euros.		✓

GDPR requires data to be kept for no longer than is necessary, it does not suggest a number of years.

The maximum fine is €20m or 4% of global turnover, whichever is higher, so may be considerably more than €20m.

(e) Identify which quality of a service is described in each of the following statements.
(4 marks)

	Intangibility	Inseparability	Variability	Perishability
It is hard to assess the quality of a service in advance	✓			
Services cannot be stored for sale in the future				✓
The quality of a service depends on who delivers it			✓	
It is hard to separate provision and consumption of a service		✓		

(f) Identify the funding source that each of the following statements relates to. **(2 marks)**

Statement	Working Capital	Loan	Equity
Glau Ltd could consider cutting the dividend.			✓
Most suitable for short term funding of inventory.	✓		

KAPLAN PUBLISHING

TASK 4 (10 MARKS)

(a) (i) Discuss which ethical principles are potentially compromised here. **(4 marks)**

> The ethical principles potentially affected are as follows:
>
> Integrity – How will B manage their personal interest with the need to be true and fair? (1 mark)
>
> Objectivity – How will B manage their personal interest in the benefits package with the need to remain unbiased and consider only the relevant facts? (1 mark)
>
> Professional Competence and Due Care – Does B have all the necessary skills to draw up such a package? (1 mark)
>
> Professional Behaviour – How should B proceed so as not to be discredited and/or discredit the accountancy profession? (1 mark)
>
> It would be very easy for B's recommendations to appear biased, even if they have acted ethically. (1 mark)

(ii) Explain what steps B should take in response to the threats identified above. **(4 marks)**

> B should start by considering the following issues:
>
> **Identify relevant facts:**
>
> They should consider the organisation's policies, procedures and guidelines, accounting standards, best practices, code of ethics, applicable laws and regulations. (1 mark)
>
> Is the information used for assessing the potential new benefits package independent? Who else has been involved in the proposal for the new benefits package? (1 mark)
>
> **Identify affected parties:**
>
> Key affected parties are B, other senior managers and the partners. (1 mark)
>
> **Identify who should be involved in the resolution:**
>
> B should consider not just who should be involved, but also for what reason and timing of their involvement. (1 mark)
>
> B could think about contacting the AAT for advice and guidance, or discuss the matter with trusted colleagues or someone from human resources. (1 mark)
>
> **Subsequent courses of action:**
>
> Before explaining their findings to the partners, it may be advisable for B to explain how they approached the project and who else was involved, for example, human resources. (1 mark)
>
> They should declare a conflict of interest and not vote on the proposal for the new benefits package. (1 mark)
>
> It may be advisable to involve human resources or another independent party to present the findings to the partners. During the presentation, B should demonstrate how the findings were arrived at and who else was involved in the project. (1 mark)

ANSWERS TO MOCK ASSESSMENT QUESTIONS: **SECTION 4**

(b) (i) What offence has D potentially committed? (1 mark)

	✓
Breach of confidentiality	
Tipping off	✓
Money laundering	
Layering	

(ii) What is the maximum prison sentence that D can receive if found guilty of the offence? (1 mark)

	✓
2 years	✓
3 years	
10 years	
14 years	

TASK 5 (10 MARKS)

(a) (i) Identify which TWO of the following events will cause a shift in the supply curve of a normal good. (2 marks)

	✓
A change in the price charged	
A change in consumer incomes	
A change in government subsidies	✓
A change in raw material costs	✓

A change in price will cause a movement along the curve but will not move the curve itself.

(ii) Identify the effect of the rise in the price of S on the quantity demanded of N, as shown on its demand curve. Select ONE option. (1 mark)

	✓
There will be a movement down the demand curve	
The demand curve will shift to the right	✓
The demand curve will shift to the left	
There will be a movement up the demand curve	

A rise in the price will cause consumers to switch to buy more N, even without a change in price of N. Thus the demand curve must have shifted to the right.

KAPLAN PUBLISHING

AAT: BUSINESS AWARENESS

(iii) Identify which TWO of the following will be the impact of the collapse and subsequent purchase of Highfashion plc. **(2 marks)**

	✓
Lower prices for high street fashion clothing as a result of reduced competition due to fewer participants.	
Heavy discounting from other online fashion retailers as a competitive response to protect their market share.	✓
Potentially unethical behaviour as other fashion retailers respond by putting more pressure on suppliers to cut prices.	✓
Increased market share for other online fashion retailers, which will lead to increased economies of scale.	

Reduced high street competition is more likely to result in price rises. Other online retailers will not see an increase in market share as Highfashion plc sold via physical stores.

(b) (i) Complete the following statement about the meaning of sustainability by selecting ONE option. **(1 mark)**

Options	✓
aims to grow is a consistent manner	
aims to reduce its carbon footprint	
meets the needs of the present	✓

(ii) Identify ONE type of sustainability that each of the following organisational policies relates to. **(3 marks)**

	Social sustainability	Environmental sustainability	Financial sustainability
"Use offsetting schemes to compensate for emission of greenhouse gases (e.g. schemes to plant additional trees somewhere else)."		✓	
"Pay taxes without finding loopholes to avoid them."			✓
"Invest in people over the long term by fostering diversity, providing challenging and exciting work and development opportunities, and rewarding for performance."	✓		

(iii) Identify whether the following statement is TRUE or FALSE. **(1 mark)**

	True	False
Trying to achieve better sustainability will inevitably increase costs and reduce profits.		✓

Sustainability may improve profit, say by reducing energy usage and lowering costs.

TASK 6 (13 MARKS)

(a) Prepare a response to Sam and Juliana in which you:

(i) Discuss the performance of the business over the six months to 30 June 20X2 and the expected performance of the business for the next six months. **(11 marks)**

Performance for the six months to 30 June 20X2

- Sales revenue and customer numbers are increasing month on month.
- Sales for both food and drinks are increasing each month.
- Restaurant A has the highest number of customers, which might indicate it was the company's first restaurant.
- The sales mix of drinks to food is reasonably constant each month.
- Revenue for restaurants A and C is increasing each month.
- Revenue for restaurant B fell from February to March.
- This is at the same time restaurant C opened, so it is likely some customers who would have gone to B went to C instead, depending on relative locations.
- After this revenue for restaurant B started to increase again, albeit slowly.
- Restaurant C has quickly grown to be larger than restaurant B, although growth seems to be slowing in recent months.

Expected performance for the next six months

- Overall sales revenue could continue to increase in the upward trend which has established over the last 6 months, although the growth does seem to be slowing, despite opening a new restaurant.
- Sales of both food and drink could continue their upward trend and the mix of products expected to stay constant.
- Restaurant A would be expected to continue to have the largest number of customers.
- Trying to predict 6 months' ahead is difficult as it will then include the Christmas period when sales are likely to be much higher due to Christmas meal bookings. Given this the trend is probably less reliable beyond, say three months.

Marks	Descriptor
0	No response worthy of credit.
1–3	The answer is not explained, or only states sales have been going up or sales at restaurant A are highest (or basic points similar to this which do not recognise there is a trend/pattern).
4–8	An answer which demonstrates a good understanding of the patterns in the data provided, where there have been upward trends in the data and where there have been decreases in performance over the six months with an attempt made to link the data from the different sources.
9–11	An answer which demonstrates a clear understanding of the patterns in the data provided, where there have been upward trends in the data and where there have been steady decreases in performance. A strong answer will link the data between the different sources, for example the increasing customers at restaurant C displacing customer numbers in other restaurants.

(ii) Identify TWO pieces of additional information which would be useful to show on the performance dashboard. **(2 marks)**

- Profits by restaurant per month (1 mark)
- Customer feedback on quality of meals (1 mark)
- Percentage of customers who come back, split by restaurant (1 mark)

TASK 7 (12 MARKS)

(a) Identify ONE appropriate strategy to deal with each of the following risks. **(2 marks)**

	Transfer	Accept	Reduce	Avoid
An open air music festival organiser is concerned about how global warming may affect the weather.		✓		
A package holiday operator is concerned about the high possibility of a civil war in country A.				✓

(b) Identify which ONE of the following factors would normally be classed as a strategic risk. **(1 mark)**

	✓
Possible obsolescence of slow moving inventory	
Problems recruiting delivery drivers	
A worldwide ban on the use of a key chemical	✓
A minor customer going bankrupt	

(c) (i) Identify which TWO of the following are benefits for Hidden Kingdom plc of having the data on ticket purchases. **(2 marks)**

	✓
Enables better staff scheduling	✓
Provides Hidden Kingdom with a range of secondary data for research	
Simplifies Hidden Kingdom's tills and operating systems	
Enables more targeted marketing efforts	✓

By identifying in advance which days are likely to be busier, staff levels can be adjusted, thus reducing cost and improving customer service.

Marketing can better target customers who have visited before by analysing when they booked and the price they paid.

ANSWERS TO MOCK ASSESSMENT QUESTIONS: **SECTION 4**

(ii) Identify the big data characteristic that underlies the challenge or benefit for Zedsa described in each statement below. **(3 marks)**

Statement	Volume	Velocity	Variety	Veracity
Data derived from shops separates out sales of 500 different products, matched to 25 shops, 125 different members of staff and the day and time of day the sales were made.			✓	
Hidden Kingdom collects and processes data from over 4 million visitors each year and monitors their activities every minute they are in the theme parks.		✓		
The on-site shop and restaurant data collection is deemed to be accurate as it is decided by and controlled by Hidden Kingdom in the systems they use.				✓

(iii) Complete the following statement about decision making by selecting ONE option. **(1 mark)**

This information will assist in making decisions about which dates to open which theme parks, so it is an example of _____ decision.

Options	✓
a strategic	
a managerial	✓
an operational	

(iv) Identify whether the following statement about the quality of the information is TRUE or FALSE. **(1 mark)**

	True	False
The information derived from social media is likely to be more reliable than that obtained from shop sales for estimating future demand.		✓

(d) Identify which TWO pieces of information Hidden Kingdom's Finance function would directly receive from the Park Operations function, not from the Human Resources function. **(2 marks)**

	✓
Ride maintenance engineer pay rise	
Overtime hours worked this week by shop staff due to sickness	✓
Changes in overtime policy for peak holiday periods	
Travel expenses due for reimbursement	✓

KAPLAN PUBLISHING